Always Making Progress

Always Making Progress

The Fundamentals of Continuous Improvement for the Process Industry

Ian Madden

CRC Press
Taylor & Francis Group
Boca Raton London New York

CRC Press is an imprint of the
Taylor & Francis Group, an **Informa** business

A PRODUCTIVITY PRESS BOOK

First published 2022
by Routledge
605 Third Avenue, New York, NY 10158

and by Routledge
2 Park Square, Milton Park, Abingdon, Oxon, OX14 4RN

Routledge is an imprint of the Taylor & Francis Group, an informa business

ISBN: 9781032155609 (hbk)
ISBN: 9781032155593 (pbk)
ISBN: 9781003244707 (ebk)

DOI: 10.4324/9781003244707

Typeset in Garamond
by Deanta Global Publishing Services, Chennai, India

To my Dad (Gerry)

Contents

List of Figures

List of Tables

Foreword

I grew up in a family business where every mealtime was a board meeting; our business is growing and packing root vegetables and potatoes. Before joining the business, I trained as an accountant. I was full of confidence as a bright young newly qualified chartered accountant and I believed, on my first day, that management was telling people what to do.

I realised within a few weeks that people hate being told what to do. There was much more to management than I thought. Our business was typical of most farming businesses in culture. A typical family farm employs a handful of people, and the owner will plan their work and instruct them each day. Our business had though evolved into a much larger business with several hundred employees, and although we were very successful, it was clear that the organisation had to change if we were going to continue to grow and thrive in a very competitive marketplace.

Washing, grading, and packing carrots are more akin to a manufacturing operation than to a typical farm. We upgraded our factories with new buildings and machinery, and we implemented a management structure with clear accountability and measurement of outcomes supported by a business-wide enterprise resource planning (ERP) system. We then addressed the central questions of how do we engage our people so that they give their discretionary effort to the business and how can we motivate them to want to be more efficient, improve quality, improve customer experience every day? We summarised this to 'how do we implement a sustainable continuous improvement culture?'

Supplying supermarkets with high-quality root vegetables and potatoes all year round is a tough business with very short lead times and a demanding pace of work. Our Packhouse colleagues were busy for 52 weeks of the year just satisfying this daily demand and, as they saw it, there was not a lot of time left to do any improvement work!

We hired Ian Madden who undertook a business analysis that showed us a way that we could implement a Continuous Improvement culture and save money at the same time. Although we retained a level of scepticism, we commissioned Ian to show us how.

Ian trained and coached our line leaders and supervisors in Continuous Improvement. It starts with a system of measuring safety, quality, delivery, cost (productivity) and morale. Then he trained them to regularly review performance in team meetings (hourly to weekly!). Line leaders were held accountable for results and were helped to understand why the results were good or not so good. By understanding the cause of good or bad performance, they became better at influencing performance. I sat in on some of the review meetings and you could see the high performers grow taller when they came to talk about their figures. After following this ritual for a few weeks, all the numbers were trending upwards.

What was interesting was that people were really enjoying the work because they were seeing their own success and they were getting recognition for that success. We were giving them the tools and understanding to do a good job and grow in confidence.

He then extended the training and coaching to our farming colleagues and worked with the senior leadership team in developing a process for more effectively deploying our strategy at all levels of the business. The business results were impressive, but more importantly for me was that the culture had changed.

A great quote from Jon Pollard, our former Business Unit director for carrots: 'we have discovered that with every pair of hands we get a free brain,' i.e. we were encouraging everyone to think for themselves and to work out how to improve future performance. The enthusiasm for going the extra mile was palpable.

It is my very strong view that nobody comes to work to do a bad job. The key to management is agreeing on goals and objectives but leaving the employees to come up with the how. So don't tell them what to do, but do agree on the targets and outcomes beforehand. The why is also important. Why is this organisation worthy of my full attention and endeavour?

Ian Madden is a hands-on passionate trainer in Continuous Improvement. He is understated and wants the team he is working with to take all the credit for great performance. This book will help you use his approach and get your employees coming to work to find ways of improving their performance day in, day out.

William Burgess
Chairman
Produce World Group

Acknowledgements

The process of writing this book has highlighted how fortunate I have been to work for and with an extraordinary list of people. I am also grateful for the guidance and support my friends and colleagues gave me during the writing process. I would like to thank, in no particular order:

Richard Moseley: For supporting and encouraging my ideas on process design specification and feedforward control.

Steve Palmer: Helped me understand the need to be practical and pragmatic and to focus on what is really needed.

Nick Meakin: Gave me the real story on what it took to be an effective operations manager.

Terry Wilson: An extraordinary thinker who introduced me to the power of workforce empowerment.

Peter Bowen: For guiding me in his innovative approach of achieving organisational performance improvement through giving frontline people the skills to manage and improve their own variance.

Alan Edwards: Gave me the real story on what it took to be an effective management consultant. He is also the most tenacious person I have ever met!

Dave Heslop, Mark Fenton, Clive Turner: For being my 'oppos' and their kind guidance on the contents of this book.

Allen Murphy, Simon Weller, Mike Andrews, Chris Antcliffe, Ray McCarthy, Reg Stewart, Rick Saini, Anna Fisher, Steve Claxton, Kevin Clayton: First-class improvement experts who are always generous with their guidance and assistance.

Manny Ajala: A fellow CI expert who gave me invaluable advice on the writing process.

Pawel Ragan: Taught me the criticality of the design of visual management and the 'power of the (dry wipe) pen'. Also for his perceptive insights on the draft manuscript.

Noel Keegan: For showing me how to navigate and deliver effective continuous improvement initiatives within a big corporate set-up with a sense of humour!

Simpson Ovans: Showed how patient focus on organisational inputs and processes can deliver extraordinary results. Also for his insightful comments on how I should approach this book.

Grant Beverley: For his support on developing ideas on how to communicate and implement truly effective strategy deployment.

Claudius Cole: Lean Six Sigma expert and training company owner who is always helpful and supportive of my efforts.

Ross O'Hara: One of the leading head brewers in the UK who, in addition to great beer, also gave me some great advice on the contents of this book.

My clients: Too many to mention for teaching me more than I have taught you.

Cheryl Madden: For her advice on the manuscript and for creating illustrations for many of the figures.

Cheryl, Sarah and Jade: For their love and support and for not letting me take myself too seriously.

Author Biography: Who Is Ian Madden?

Ian has a passion for all things to do with Continuous Improvement driven by the significant benefits it can bring to people and the organisations they work for. His interest is in helping teams achieve sustainable behavioural changes to improve operational effectiveness.

Graduating in 1985 with a degree in chemical engineering, he has spent over 35 years in process engineering, project engineering, operations management up to Operations Director level and Continuous Improvement. The last 20 years have been spent as a Continuous Improvement Practitioner both as a consultant and as an in-house Continuous Improvement Manager. In 2015, Ian set up Torrs Consulting Ltd (www.torrsconsulting.com), a Continuous Improvement consulting company providing services to industrial and service organisations.

During his career, he has worked for or provided services to over 130 organisations in both the UK and overseas in Consumer Packaged Goods, Pharmaceuticals, Automotive, Health Care, Farming, Retail and General Manufacturing including Mondelez (Cadbury), Nestlé, Akzo Nobel, Hain Daniels, Greene King, Rolls Royce, Produce World, New Covent Garden Soup Company, National Health Service, Riverford Organic Farmers, Greencore and Irish Distillers.

He has a deep knowledge of Continuous Improvement tools and techniques developed from achieving Master Black Belt level and his extensive experience. His projects have covered many functional areas including manufacturing, maintenance, project engineering, warehousing and distribution, planning, procurement, new product introduction, laboratory processes, farming, health and safety, and hospital and General Practitioner operations.

Ian lives in North Devon, UK.

Chapter 1

Introduction

> If you're going to do something, go start. Life's simpler than we
> sometimes can admit.
>
> **Robert De Niro**

If you are looking for a practical, straight to the point guide on how to start
and get better at **Continuous Improvement** (CI), then this manual will
be useful. Specifically, it is a Continuous Improvement fundamental 'how
to guide' primarily aimed at people who work within processing industries
such as food and drink, consumer-packaged goods, ingredients, packaging
and pharmaceuticals.

It will be of particular interest to those working in or aspiring to work in
the following disciplines:

- General Management
- Production
- Continuous Improvement Practitioner/Consultant
- Technical/Quality Assurance
- Engineering
- Supply Chain (Purchasing, Planning and Logistics)
- New Product Development
- Health, Safety and Environment

Within the manual, 'Operations' is mentioned – please note this is a collec-
tive term for all the above.

DOI: 10.4324/9781003244707-1

For those of you in positions of senior leadership, whose sponsorship of Continuous Improvement is a vital factor in its success and sustainability, it is important to state, from the outset, that this manual's approach is unashamedly 'bottom up' as opposed to 'top down,' i.e. starting small and developing the approach from there. The last chapter of the manual is **Skills and Culture Development**, a fundamental enabler of each stage of the Continuous Improvement Journey. Please read it first if you would like guidance on how to create the right environment and facilitate CI cultural development. The chapters are sequenced in a 'bottom-up' order however, as the Continuous Improvement Journey is a cycle, it is possible to start at any point.

The manual is structured in a way that you can use it to guide you by implementing the basic foundations of CI through to an organisation where Continuous Improvement is a 'way of life' and a defining feature of the culture of the organisation.

In your role, you may have many pressing concerns such as:

- Elimination of accidents and near misses
- Reducing customer complaints
- Improving customer delivery performance
- Introducing new products
- Improving staff productivity
- Removing costs to meet budget
- Dealing with absence and poor morale
- Improving staff retention

This manual will provide you with guidance on how to address issues in these areas in a way that enables improvements to be realised quickly but not at the expense of a long-term goal of a sustainable Continuous Improvement culture.

What this guide will not do is provide you with an end point. As represented in Figure 1.1, the very nature of Continuous Improvement is that it is never ending as we are always journeying towards but never achieving perfection. Toyota, arguably the world's greatest manufacturer and exponent of Continuous Improvement, has been on its journey for well over 75 years and is still striving to increase the value to its customers and improve the way it does things.

Continuous Improvement is a vast subject with many takes on principles, approaches and tools. This manual is about how all the fundamentals of

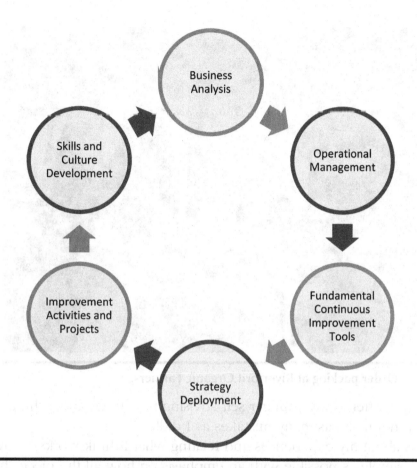

Figure 1.1   The never-ending Continuous Improvement Journey.

these areas fit together and, as such, covers only some of them. However, within the bibliography, I have signposted the books that have guided me during my career and which go into the principles, approaches and tools in more detail.

You may have come across terms such as Lean Manufacturing and Six Sigma and the various merits of each. Within this manual, I refer to both and pick out what I think works.

Sometimes people who undertake Continuous Improvement have a job title that includes one of the following terms: 'Operational Excellence,' 'Business Improvement,' 'Black Belt,' 'Transformation,' 'Scrum,' 'Agile,' etc.

Is any job title better than another? Who knows? In my opinion, there is one overriding 'job title' that Continuous Improvement applies to and that is 'human being.'

I have spent over 35 years working in the processing industries in engineering, operations management and consultancy roles. This manual is

Figure 1.2   Order packing at Riverford Organic Farmers.

essentially a letter to my younger self advising how to go about things and, hopefully, not make as many mistakes as I did!

As it is about my experiences and relating what I think works, I have kept it as simple as possible with an emphasis on how all the pieces fit together. My style has been described as personable and pragmatic and I have tried to come across as 'me.' Consequently, I have written a lot of it in the first person and tried to reduce the amount of jargon. My motto is 'don't let perfect get in the way of better.' This manual, I hope, conveys this and the spirit of 'Always Making Progress.'

Continuous Improvement is fascinating as there is always something new to learn on the journey.

Enjoy the ride!

Be curious, not judgmental

Walt Whitman

Chapter 2

How This Manual Is Structured

I keep six honest serving men

(They taught me all I knew);

Their names are What and Why and When

And How and Where and Who.

Rudyard Kipling

2.1 Always Making Progress

Put simply, Continuous Improvement is about changing how things are done to achieve better outcomes and *to keep doing this*. We could describe it in more everyday terms as 'Always Making Progress.' This may be for yourself, your family, your community, your team, your company, your country, the planet etc.

Making progress is similar to going on a journey; you are at place A; you need or want to go to place B and you have the means and opportunity to make the journey. The 'checklist' for a successful journey is provided in Table 2.1.

Any box that is a 'no' will probably mean that, at best, satisfactory progress is not made and, at worst, complete failure. To quote Henry Ford:

Most people aim for nothing in their lives and hit the target with immaculate precision.

DOI: 10.4324/9781003244707-2

Table 2.1 Continuous Improvement Checklist

Item	Comments	Achieved (Yes or No?)
Situation	An awareness of where you are now and any shortfalls.	
Motive	There is desire to leave where you are now and go to where you want to be.	
Destination	Know where you are going: The 'target condition.'	
Capability	Have the means and opportunity to get there: Resources, time, skills and tools.	
Route map	Plan the work, work the plan.	

Many approaches to Continuous Improvement do not cover the whole journey. In particular, many focus on the skills and tools aspect with little regard to the other areas. For me, this would be like training an athlete how to improve her skills but then not monitor and coach her performance (situation), have no championships to qualify and win at (motive), have no medals to aim for (destination) and have no training plan (route map).

This manual takes these items into account at each stage of the Continuous Improvement Journey as they have to be there so that we can be 'Always Making Progress.'

2.2 How Do All the Pieces Fit Together?

Dr W. Edwards Deming (1900–1993) was an American engineer, statistician, professor, author, lecturer and management consultant who is widely credited as playing a significant role in the development of Continuous Improvement thinking and approaches, particularly in Japan. He is also my hero when it comes to Continuous Improvement. Here are some of his quotes:

> Each system is perfectly designed to give you exactly what you are getting today.
> If you can't describe what you are doing as a process, you don't know what you're doing.

85% of the reasons for failure are deficiencies in the systems and process rather than the employee. The role of management is to change the process rather than badgering individuals to do better.

There is a bit of a theme here isn't there? It is the systems and processes that people work in that achieve results, and it is the design of the systems and processes that is the primary driver for how effective the organisation is, not the people who work in them.

> Put a good person in a bad system and the bad system wins, no contest.

In my experience, this is **the most important thing** to understand and accept about organisational effectiveness and its Continuous Improvement. I will discuss this more later in Chapter 4.

There are many system models that have been developed to describe how 'all the pieces fit together' which so-called Continuous Improvement experts like me love to discuss the relative merits of. This is the one that I use (Figure 2.1).

I like it because apart from mentioning trains, it provides a very coherent process system for linking inputs and desired outcomes.

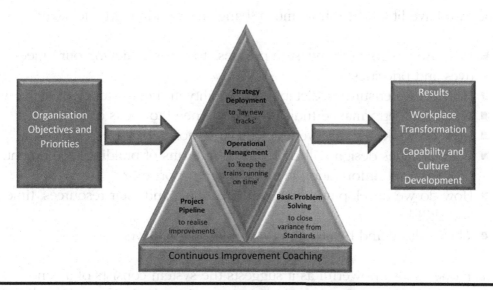

Figure 2.1   Organisational model for a Continuous Improvement system.

2.2.1 Inputs: Organisational Objectives and Priorities

What is the spark that lights the fuse? Continuous Improvement does not happen in a vacuum. There must be a reason that the organisation, team or individual is undertaking it.

- What are our principles?
- What do we need to do to survive and prosper in a way that is in line with our principles?
- Where do we get the information to develop our strategy?
- What is our SWOT (Strengths, Weaknesses, Opportunities and Threats)?
- How do we arrive at and define the mission in terms of objectives and scope?
- How do we communicate the strategy and get everyone on board?
- Are we focusing on one issue in one area or are we considering a 'wall to wall, floor to ceiling' approach across the whole organisation?
- How do we prioritise the work and define the 'vital few' priorities to work on?
- How do we ensure the strategy is delivered?

2.2.2 Outcomes: Results, Workplace Transformation and Capability and Culture Development

Once we have lit the fuse how much 'bang' are we aiming to achieve?

- How are we going to measure progress towards achieving our objectives and priorities?
- How do we ensure predictability, reliability and consistency of delivery?
- What Key Performance Indicators do we need to focus on?
- How do we know that we are achieving those objectives?
- What facilities design will be required in terms of building, equipment, process plant, information technology, transport etc.?
- How do we develop and manage our people and their resources, time and skills?
- What culture and behaviours do we wish to achieve?

This model is also powerful as it suggests the system consists of a central core that links the future with the present, like the two cogs shown in Figure 2.2.

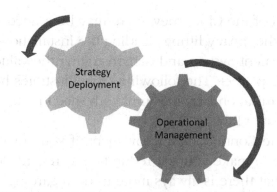

Figure 2.2   Strategy deployment and operational management.

Operational Management: Firstly, it is about **delivering** the right things today and keeping our promises: 'Keep the trains running on time.'

Strategy Deployment: Secondly, it is about **keeping** winning in the market place by focusing improvements on the organisation's priorities: 'Lay new tracks and build new stations.'

2.2.3 *Continuous Improvement Coaching*

The last part of the system is where this manual comes in. Building capability should always be about giving the people who do the job the skills to improve the job. The role of the Continuous Improvement Practitioner is ultimately about skills transfer not doing Continuous Improvement (CI).

When I set out to write this manual, I asked myself: is the target audience Operational roles or CI Practitioners? The latter can be further categorised into internal specialists or external consultants. I decided it should be everybody who should do CI, i.e. everybody in the organisation.

It is not all about knowledge transfer, the very fact that Practitioners are used in an organisation is partly driven by the inability of operational people to do the work whilst having a 'day job.' Many operational managers have some of these skills but not the time, they believe, to put anything into action. There were many occasions in my early consulting career when we went in and created a programme with internal training and coaching as part of the remit only to be called back again as it had slipped off as soon as we had left. The key to preventing this is for everyone to agree that the Skills and Culture Development aspect *is the ultimate goal* as opposed to just short-term results. If the latter threatens the former, then of course, it can be done, but it is not Continuous Improvement.

In the early days of the CI journey, there may be a need for CI Practitioners to do the 'heavy lifting': leading the installation of an Operations Management System and demonstrating the value of CI in delivering a specific project. The following table illustrates how the CI role develops as an organisation becomes more advanced in its Continuous Improvement maturity (Table 2.2).

So, for sustainable Continuous Improvement, if you are a CI Practitioner, your aim should be to make yourself redundant as regards 'doing CI' – the good news is that there is always more to do regarding 'training and

Table 2.2   Roles and Responsibilities during the Continuous Improvement Journey

Stage of Journey	Level	Activity	CI Role
Foundation	Operation	Business analysis	CI Practitioner
	Operation	Operations management facilitation	CI Practitioner
	Area	Improvement project	Operations Leaders
Intermediate	Area	Operations management facilitation	Operations Leaders
	Operation	CI programme and tools facilitation	CI Practitioner
	Operation	Business analysis	Site Leaders
	Area	Improvement projects	Frontline Leaders
	Site	Strategy deployment facilitation	CI Practitioner
Advanced	Area	Operations management facilitation	Frontline Managers
	Operation	CI programme and tools facilitation	Operations Leaders
	Operation	Business analysis	Operations Leaders
	Area	Improvement projects	Everyone
	Site	Strategy deployment facilitation	Site Leaders
	Enterprise	Skills and culture development	CI Practitioner

coaching CI.' You are a service provider and your customer is the operational team. If you are in the operational team, your aim should be to make CI 'part of the day job' and 'the way we do things around here.' Treat authentic Continuous Improvement Practitioners with respect and trust as they are there to help you. Make time for their work. They will challenge you, be able to see things with a 'fresh pair of eyes' and ultimately help you and your team to have more fulfilling and rewarding work. After all, who wants to go to work and solve the same problems every day!

> Funny how we don't have time to improve but we have plenty of time to perform work inefficiently and to resolve the same problems over and over.
>
> **W. Edwards Deming**

2.3 Leadership

One way to look at the impact of leadership on Continuous Improvement is to look at the main reasons why most Continuous Improvement initiatives ultimately fail within the framework of the 'Always Making Progress' checklist shown earlier (Table 2.3).

Table 2.3 Continuous Improvement Checklist with Reasons for Failure

Item	Comments	Reason for Failure
Situation	An awareness of where you are now and any shortfalls.	No feedback loop.
Motive	There is desire to leave where you are now and/or go to where you want to be.	No leadership support. Too much, too quick. 'Flavour of the Month.'
Destination	Know where you are going: the 'target condition.'	Failure to engage and involve employees in improvement.
Capability	Have the means and opportunity to get there: Resources, time, skills and tools.	Too much focus on the tools. No focused training.
Route map	Plan the work, work the plan.	We don't 'stick at' our strategy. We don't have time to do CI. CI is a low priority.

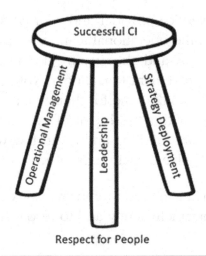

Figure 2.3   The critical elements of successful Continuous Improvement.

All these failures can be bracketed under 'Leadership Failure,' in fact, in my experience, Continuous Improvement **only** fails where there is poor leadership. The following diagram is a good representation of the impact. If you take one of the legs of the stool away the whole thing 'falls over' (Figure 2.3):

Whilst this manual is not a Leadership guide per se; leadership is interwoven through all the steps described in the following chapters. Its importance cannot be over emphasised.

2.4 Respect for People

For successful CI, the answers to the following (non-exhaustive) list **have to be** yes.

- Is the organisation genuinely interested in helping people be the best that they can be?
- Does the organisation develop its people?
- Does the organisation believe that most people want to do a good job?
- If things go wrong, it is not the organisation's first instinct to look who to blame?
- Is bad behaviour 'called out' and acted upon, i.e. not ignored or 'brushed over?'

- Do employees always treat others in the way they would wish to be treated?
- Are people able to give honest respectful feedback when someone has failed in their duties or conduct?
- Are people able to 'blow the whistle' without fear of retribution?
- If team members ask their leaders questions or make requests they are always given a respectful answer and never silence.

Think about the above, if there are any negatives, **there is work to be done.**

2.5 The Continuous Improvement Journey

This manual provides guidance on the fundamentals needed to move through the various stages of the Continuous Improvement Journey. This is a summary of the following chapters (Figure 2.4).

3. **Business Analysis**
   How to review the current situation, highlight the opportunities and arrive at a plan to realise those opportunities.
4. **Operations Management Facilitation**
   How to design, implement and install an effective operational management system so that the performance is predictable, reliable and consistent on a daily basis.
5. **Fundamental Continuous Improvement Tools**
   Guidance on how to choose what Continuous Improvement tool is needed for a particular circumstance and how to use them.
6. **Strategy Deployment Facilitation**
   How to design, implement and install an effective Strategy Deployment System so that the objectives and priorities of the organisation can be delivered.

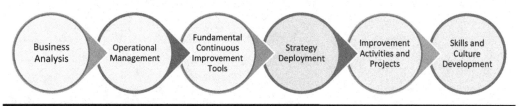

Figure 2.4   The Continuous Improvement Journey.

7. **Improvement Activities and Projects**

How to determine and deliver an effective Continuous Improvement plan and projects on a Site and/or Area level with guidance on more advanced tools.

8. **Skills and Culture Development**

A discussion of the factors impacting skills and culture within an organisation:

Bibliography

Recommended further reading. Signposting the books that have influenced me the most and provide further reading and guidance.

Chapter 3

Business Analysis

I'll often joke that when people ask 'What is business analysis?,' I say: 'You know all those times that people say, "somebody should look into that?" I'm the person who looks into that.'

Jen Neuls

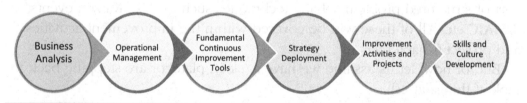

Figure 3.1 Business analysis.

3.1 Why Are Business Analyses Undertaken?

You have to start somewhere, don't you? In this chapter, we will review how Continuous Improvement typically starts within an organisation. As we will see, the reasons for wanting a performance improvement are often prosaic as opposed to profound, but, nonetheless, the followings steps are universal:

a. Stakeholder(s) namely owner, director, manager, employee, union, trustee, official, politician, specialists etc. within the organisation have an awareness that the current performance is not meeting, or at some point in the future will not meet, requirements. Alternatively, there may be just a desire that 'we need to improve but don't know how to do this.'

DOI: 10.4324/9781003244707-3

b. The stakeholders investigate it, or someone is asked to investigate it and come back with findings and recommendations.
c. The stakeholder or someone carries out the analysis and reports back.
d. The stakeholders decide what to do next which may be to do nothing.
e. The stakeholders act based on the recommendations.

In later chapters, we will see that in a highly developed Continuous Improvement organisation, the steps mentioned above are in the cultural 'DNA' of everyone in the organisation, and it is an activity that happens at all stages of the Continuous Improvement Journey and, indeed, as a key part of normal day-to-day activity.

Within strategy deployment (Chapter 6), there is an explanation of an ongoing business analysis and governance process which ensures that the step change and directional change improvement initiatives of the organisation are linked with the organisation's priorities.

Value stream mapping is a well-known multidisciplinary diagnostic approach for identifying the 'current state,' the non-value-adding waste within an organisation and a 'future state.' 'Problem definition' is also a key part of structured problem-solving techniques such as 'A3,' 'Kaizen events,' 'DMAIC etc. All of these will be covered within the improvement activities and project (Chapter 7).

But for now, let us assume we have a 'clean plate' or are stepping back to look at things afresh.

3.2 What Is a Business Analysis?

Business analysis is a structured process to review the whole or part of an organisation's current situation, highlight the opportunities and arrive at a plan to realise those opportunities. It is normally quite short in duration (1–2 weeks). For an analysis to be effective, there need to be data available and the data need to be sound.

Within the Continuous Improvement consulting world, it is often the first stage of engagement with a client where the analysis team is essentially 'measuring up' for a larger project. They are aiming to convince the client that the solutions proposed by the consultants will solve the client's problems and realise the benefits indicated. In this way, it is as much a selling process as an operational study (Figure 3.1)

3.3 When Is a Business Analysis Undertaken?

There are a multitude of triggers. Typically, a senior leader is concerned with performance or wants to realise an opportunity within part or the whole organisation. He then wants to develop a plan to resolve this. He would then ask somebody either within the company or a consulting organisation to look into it. Often it is an urgent priority as opposed to an important long-term need that triggers this type of activity. There follow some examples of 'problems' (issues/opportunities) that I have worked on in the past:

3.3.1 Safety

Increasing total accident frequency rate.

3.3.2 Quality

High internal batch failure leading to loss of capacity and high waste.
High numbers of process deviations within a pharmaceutical company leading to poor throughput.
Poor external customer experience (e.g. high levels of complaints).

3.3.3 Delivery

Increasing sales requiring rapid production capacity increases.
Poor customer service levels.
Delivery shortages leading to loss of a major customer.
Very high back-order situation.
Long lead times to market and problematic product launches.
Poor equipment availability and performance of maintenance team.

3.3.4 Cost

High costs owing to having to run a factory 24 hours 7 days a week to meet customer demand.
Excessive storage costs and high working capital owing to poor forecast and scheduling process.
High labour costs owing to poor line performance and labour control.

Late running and overspent capital project.
High ingredients' wastage levels in food factory.
High transportation costs because of poor utilisation of vehicles.
High write off and wastage costs for packaging procurement and use.
Requirement for a profit improvement plan to get back on budget.

3.3.5 Morale

High labour turnover and poor skills level.
Poor accountability and ownership of performance.
Lack of personal development planning.
High degree of variability in people's performance and behaviour.
Poor morale and performance focus.
Poor role definition, structure and competency development.
Lack of ownership of asset care by frontline teams.

3.3.6 Organisation/Site

Look at things with a 'fresh pair of eyes' and indicate where we could
  improve.
Need for a site-prioritised Continuous Improvement (CI) plan.
Need for a strategy deployment plan.
A desire to implement a sustainable Continuous Improvement culture.
Benchmarking exercise.

3.4 Where Is a Business Analysis Undertaken?

Within most processing companies, there are normally four broad areas of
operation that analyses are undertaken with the majority being focused on
value-added processes:

■ **Value-added processes** are frontline processes that create value for
  the customer. Value is defined as a service/product/feature that a customer is willing to pay for and is typically 'direct' costs to the organisation that impacts gross margin. The type of process will also be defined
  on where it sits on the continuum shown below, e.g. a sandwich company supplying the multiple retailers will normally use an 'Assembly

PROCESS SELECTION CONTINUUM				
PROJECT	JOBBING	BATCH	ASSEMBLY	CONTINUOUS
One off activities to customer specification	Repeat activities to customer specification	Repeat activities to customer options	Repeat activities to standard specification	Continuous activities to standard specification

Figure 3.2 Process continuum.

Process,' whereas a chemical company will use a 'Continuous Process' (See Figure 3.2).

■ **Support processes** include Planning and Scheduling, Logistics, Maintenance, Hygiene, Health, Safety and Environment, Human Resources, IT etc. Typically, these are overhead costs.

■ **Audit processes** include Finance and Quality Assurance.

■ **Business and commercial processes** include Marketing, New Product Development, Sales, Business Development etc.

These are some examples of business areas that I have undertaken a business analysis:

■ Filling and packing
■ Assembly
■ Packaging processes
■ Ingredients processing
■ Raw material preparation and waste control
■ Mixing and blending
■ Fermentation
■ Cooking and other forms of heat treatment
■ Sales order forecasting, planning and scheduling
■ Farming operations
■ Distribution warehousing and transport
■ Research and development
■ Customer service
■ Laboratories and QA
■ New product development
■ Engineering project management
■ Engineering maintenance
■ Environmental impacts

3.5 Who Undertakes a Business Analysis?

Analyses are normally led by experienced internal or external Continuous Improvement practitioners. It is important to adopt a consultant mindset even if you work within the operation on a day-to-day basis:

- I am external (even if I am not in my 'usual role') to the team and will evaluate the issue(s) without any preconceived bias or fear or favour.
- I will treat the analysis as a distinct piece of work that has specified outcomes.
- I will be professional and treat people with respect and courtesy.
- Relationships are vital – I will actively build and nurture these during the analysis.
- My pace of work and approach with the client team will create a sense of urgency.
- My recommendations will be based on data and facts only and be rigorous.
- Ongoing communication with the client team is crucial to ensure that the analysis 'course corrects' depending on findings, and the ultimate findings are not a surprise to them.
- High standards of presentation and communication are a cornerstone of my work.
- I want to secure the next stage, as if I don't, I will fail commercially.

3.5.1 Roles

3.5.1.1 Client

Usually, a Senior Manager is responsible and accountable for the area in which the problem is occurring. He is often called the 'Sponsor.'

3.5.1.2 Senior Continuous Improvement Manager

Please note this role and the following three roles may all be the same person! The roles here are split as may be the case in a larger consultancy company. The *Senior Continuous Improvement Manager* is the senior CI expert who runs the wider consulting team and is accountable for quality and delivery of the service being provided.

3.5.1.3 Account Director

This is the person who carries out the initial selling of the work. Her day-to-day responsibilities are the commercial activities: marketing, identifying new clients and ongoing account management and retention.

3.5.1.4 Analysis Manager

He is the person carrying out the analysis work either on his own or with a team.

3.5.1.5 Finance Director

He is responsible to ensure that the work being provided has been costed correctly to ensure a reasonable return on the work, plus ensuring that all legal, contractual and risk management considerations have been fully considered and incorporated into the proposal before it is presented to the Client.

3.6 How Are Business Analyses Undertaken?

The following describes how an analysis can be undertaken by an external Continuous Improvement practitioner, in this scenario the practitioner ('Analysis Manager') does not have any or only limited knowledge of the *Client* and problem being addressed. The process will be applicable to 'internal personnel' who may have detailed knowledge of the problem area. As it is important not to jump to conclusions and avoid biased thinking, it is recommended that the process is followed in full no matter if you are internal or external and have limited or detailed experience of the 'problem area' (Figure 3.3).

The greyed out areas relate to activities carried out on the client's site.

3.6.1 Scoping Review

In the 'why' section earlier, I described several triggers that could start the analysis. Before starting, though it is important to determine the likely scope of the problem as this will help you understand the problem in more depth,

Step	Finance Director	Account Director	Analysis Manager	Senior CI Manager	Client
1					Analysis Request
2		Brief Analysis Manager	Scoping Review		Site Information
3		Prepare Proposal			
4	Proposal Approval				
5		Liaise with Client			Agreement to go ahead
6			Ensure Checklist Completed		
7			Source and Brief Team	Advice on CI Practitioner Availability	
9			Raise Draft Plan		
10			Agree Plan with Client		Agreement at 'Kick off' Meeting
11			Ensure Plan Completed		Site Liaison and Support
12			Ensure Report Completed		
13	Approve Proposal	Approve Proposal			
14		Attend Review Meeting	Present Proposal Report		Final Review Meeting
15	Approve Terms	Negotiate Terms			Agreement to go ahead
16		Identify Project Resource		Advice on CI Practitioner Availability	
17			Carry out Handover	Attend Handover	
18				Initiate Project	

Figure 3.3   Overall analysis process.

pinpoint the areas in which to undertake the analysis and identify a plan for delivering the analysis.

In discussions with the *Client*, the *Account Director* would have determined the outline details of what is required by the *Client*. The *Analysis Manager's* task is now to firm up these details by either discussing it further with the *Client* or, if possible, visiting the site and walking the area under consideration.

'Gemba' is the Japanese word that means 'Actual Place,' and the term is often used within Continuous Improvement to describe 'where the real work takes place.' If possible, go to the Gemba to scope out the analysis. By walking the area, observing activities for yourself and talking to the people by asking the open questions shown in the following '5W2H' table in the area, you will get a much better appreciation of both the area and the issue.

For each question, it is important to determine 'is' and 'is not' to enable you to pinpoint the area under consideration and not to be distracted by other issues that are not important to the problem being considered (Table 3.1).

3.6.2 Prepare Proposal

Following the scoping review, a proposal can be prepared by the *Account Director* that sets out:

- ▪ **Client Brief**
    - What is the main issue/opportunity under consideration?
    - What is the desired future state that the client wants following an improvement programme?
    - Confirm that the analysis will enable an improvement programme to be determined to achieve the desired future state with a cost–benefit analysis.
- ▪ **Details**
    - How long will the analysis take and how much resource will be required (man-days of analysis time)?
    - An outline plan with proposed start dates.
    - Data set: A request for historical data and other information to be provided prior to the analysis starting.
    - Cost of the programme if this is relevant.

The 'go-ahead' decision is then sought from the *Client* and the planning starts in earnest.

Table 3.1 **Scoping Questions**

5W2H	Question	Is	Is Not
What	• Specific product, line or area? • Key performance indicators are being considered? • Pattern of performance is seen? • Loss areas and categories? • The desired future state (people, process, plant)?		
Where	• Geographic location? • Position of the problem in the supply chain? • Area of the factory/organisation? • Specific Location of the problem?		
When	• When did the problem start? • When was it first noticed?		
Who	• Team structure, roles and responsibilities? • Suppliers and customers of the process • Culture of the organisation?		
How much?	• Cost of the current problem on an annualised basis? • What type of cost–benefit model is being considered? (e.g. more for the same or the same for less) • Current budget performance? • Other people/'soft' benefits being considered?		
How many?	• Current performance? • Trends? • Potential loss areas? • Future performance target? • How are KPIs measured at the moment?		

3.6.3 Final Pre-analysis Activities

3.6.3.1 Data Set

It is recommended that a request for information will be made to the *Client* before the analysis starts in order that these data are available at the start of the analysis. This is a typical list:

■ Weekly production summaries (up to a year by week if possible, minimum 3 months)
  – Complaint levels per million units
  – Units produced

- Customer service levels
- Plan adherence
- Overall equipment effectiveness
- Breakdown/downtime analysis
- Waste/rejects (with reason codes if applicable)
- Maintenance time
- Material and labour variances
- Labour, energy and any other relevant costs per unit produced
- Labour hours worked by frontline staff by department

■ Forecast sales by Stock Keeping Unit (SKU) for next 12 months
■ Crewing
  - By area/line/product (if relevant)
  - Shift and crewing plan
  - Overtime, absenteeism, agency contribution
■ Line speeds by product/size
■ Skills matrix by shift
■ Organisational chart down to operator level including support functions
■ Fixed costs breakdown
■ Variable costs breakdown
■ Maintenance tasks scheduled/completed
■ Maintenance costs.

The following checklist is used to ensure that all bases are covered (Figure 3.4).

3.6.3.2 Briefing the Team

Larger analysis may require a team of people in order to carry out the analysis plan. To determine team size, the following estimation method is recommended for a typical 2-week analysis (Table 3.2).

To illustrate:

A site with 150 people running 5 days a week with three shifts looking at quality and materials would require a team of 2.

A site with a team of 320 people with an analysis looking at labour only would require a team of 2.

A site with a team of 75 people with an analysis looking at labour only would require a team of 1.

A site with a team of 375 people with an analysis looking at labour, materials and delivery would require a team of 6.

Pre- Analysis Check list

(To be completed by Analysis Manager)

Client Company		
Key Client Contact		**Analysis Manager**
Account Director		**Key client decision maker**
No. of Man-days		**Deadline for draft report completion**
Dates of Analysis		

Objective

Scope

Analysis Personnel

	Y or N?		Y or N
Analyst briefed by Acct Director?		Report or Presentation confirmed?	
Data set sent to client?		Order placed by Client?	
Start time and contact confirmed?		Client team available?	
Hotels and PPE organised/clarified?		Analyst team Briefed?	
Man-days and team confirmed?		Dress sense confirmed?	
Draft plan completed?		Required studies identified?	
Date of presentation confimed?		Final Report format determined?	

Any other factors that should be considered?

PRE- PRESENTATION APPROVAL FOR DRAFT DOCUMENT			
Analysis Manager		**Senior CI Manager**	
SIGNATURE		SIGNATURE	
DATE		DATE	

Figure 3.4   Pre-analysis checklist.

Table 3.2 Number of Analysts Required Table

Employees in Operations (up to 24/7 Operation)	No. Analysts: Quality KPIs Under Consideration	No. Analysts: Delivery KPIs Under Consideration	No. Analysts: Labour Costs Under Consideration	No. Analysts: Materials Costs Under Consideration
<200	1			
<200		1		
<200			1	
<200				1
<400	2			
<400		2		
<400			2	
<400				2

Smaller operations of <75 people would require only an analysis lasting 1 week.

The task in hand will mean that these estimates will need to be increased on occasion; ultimately it is the analysis plan and the number of studies that are required that will dictate man-power required.

Before the analysis starts, the *Analysis Manager* will identify the team and secure their availability for the duration of the analysis and write-up. The manager would make contact with the team and brief them on the outline brief, the likely studies, and ensure study preparation (the including necessity for analysis/study templates to fill in on long observational exercises, not just a notebook) and lastly ensure travel, personal protective equipment and other housekeeping elements are adequately addressed.

3.6.4 Developing the Analysis Plan

A draft plan will normally be developed before going on site: It will indicate the review and studies that have to be undertaken to complete the analysis. A typical plan for a short analysis with one analyst is shown in Figure 3.5. For larger analyses, a plan is produced per analysis team member. The types of studies indicated are described later.

ANALYSIS PLAN		Client	An Example Ltd	Week		1 of 1
AP Manager		MONDAY 07-Mar	TUESDAY 08-Mar	WEDNESDAY 09-Mar	THURSDAY 10-Mar	FRIDAY 11-Mar
Activity 1	Scope	Site	Planning, Production, Quality, and Engineering Functions	Bottling Plant	Engineering	Site
	Objective	Gain insight into Clients needs and wants. Review data set information	Gain insights into detailed department set ups and issues that each manager perceives	Quantify losses at start up and root cause	Determine effectiveness of maintenance set up	Proposal Preparation
	Method and duration	Introductory Meeting (2 hours)	Process mapping interviews(4 x 1 hour each)	Start up study (2 hours)	Review of service completion and line availability performance	Final Write Up (2 hours)
	Contact	Site Manager and Team	Department Managers	Shift Manager	Engineering Manager	Client Board
Activity 2	Scope	Site	Bottling Plant	Line 1	Contingency	Proposal Development
	Objective	Gain awareness of factory set up and personnel	Determine flow and speeds of bottling lines and possible issues	Quantify losses and root causes of highest volume line	Contingency Study time	Ensure proposal meets commercial objectives / review operational arrangements
	Method and duration	Site Tour (3 hours)	Line Schematics and Speed Profiling (2 hours)	Line study (4 hours)	4 hours	Review meeting (1 hour)
	Contact	Department Manager and Team Leaders	Production Manager	Shift Manager and Team leader	To be determined	Account Director
Activity 3	Scope	Site	Bottling Plant	Line 5	Site	Proposal Presentation
	Objective	Determine key financial drivers and historical performance	Determine Waste flows and possible issues	Quantify possible set up time compression	Proposal Preparation	Project Approval
	Method and duration	1 to 1 Review (2 hours)	Flow charting	Changeover study (2 hours)	Final Write Up (2 hours)	2 hour presentation
	Contact	Financial Manager	Production Manager	Shift Manager and Team Leader	Client Board	Client Board

Figure 3.5   Analysis plan example.

The areas shaded are used on most analyses. The un-shaded areas will depend on the specific type of objective and the scope of the area being investigated.

A reasonable estimate for the number of study activities required per analysis is about 9 per week for the *Analysis Manager* and 12 per week for each team member.

The plan is not fixed and will be refined and adjusted as the analysis proceeds and findings indicate the areas which need to be investigated (Figure 3.5).

To explain the common sections:

■ Introductory Meeting: A 'kick off' meeting with the key client and hopefully his team to confirm the objective, scope and plan for the analysis. Team availability, access to areas and any 'housekeeping' items can also be discussed and agreed. The data set sent before the analysis can also be reviewed at this meeting.

■ Site Tour: Walking the area so that you and your team can familiarise yourself with the 'problem area.'

■ Financial Manager Review: A meeting with whoever is responsible for compiling the operation's management accounts. Historical performance, cost per units and other financial drivers can be discussed to determine the 'baseline' performance and how a cost–benefit model and underpinning rationale can be developed to illustrate the likely savings or additional revenues that any identified improvement work will generate. Generally, models follow either a SAME FOR LESS model or a MORE FOR THE SAME model. The former being applicable in areas with flat or declining demand, and the latter for areas with increasing demand growth. In line with the principles of sustainable Continuous Improvement, it is important to not focus on reducing permanent headcount as this will be detrimental to long-term sustainability. Examples of possible financial benefits:
  - Inspection, rework and scrap reduction.
  - Customer complaints reduction.
  - Overtime cost reduction.
  - Absence cost reduction.
  - Agency cost reduction.
  - Training, improvement and development time increase.

- Stock Keeping Unit rationalisation to remove unnecessary stock holding/manufacture of either components/ingredients, work in progress and finished goods.
- Yield improvement.
- Process simplification leading to lower skill requirements.
- Reduction of service and contractor costs.
- Material and packaging over usage reduction.
- Extra capacity (gross margin improvement).
- Energy and environmental loss reduction.
- Inventory costs reduction.
- Working capital reduction.
- Storage costs reduction.
- Transportation cost reduction.
- Maintenance costs reduction.
- Buildings cost reduction.
- Material and packaging cost reduction.
- Inspection, rework and scrap reduction.
- Customer complaints reduction.
- Late orders on costs (e.g. having to use express delivery).
- Capital expenditure avoidance.

Further details on how to develop a cost–benefit model within CI project management are described in Chapter 7.

3.6.5 Historical Performance Data Review

$$Y = f(X)$$

Most analyses are aiming to answer how much an 'effect' factor 'Y' represented by a key performance indicator (KPI) can be improved by changing the 'cause' factors 'X' such as people, processes and plant.

In preparing a historical performance data review, the aim is to identify each relevant KPI and then show time series plots to provide an indication of the 'baseline position.' Often the required KPI(s) are not being recorded either at all or sufficiently accurately to determine how well the operation is performed with regard to these KPI(s).

Typically, time series plots are developed from the data set that was requested (see earlier).

To illustrate baseline development, let's consider an example where the analysis is targeting a situation where 'Customer Service' (orders met vs orders placed) is falling short of requirements. One of the relevant areas to look at would be production capacity and so reviewing a KPI such as overall equipment effectiveness would be useful.

It is important to look at the data and determine the relevant baseline period. Factors such as fluctuating demand ('seasonality') and the patterns of performance are important. In the following example, we can see that performance has been trending downwards for a whole year. The optimum baseline period that should probably be considered is the last 3 months rather than the whole year as mean performance in this period is lower than the whole year (Figure 3.6).

If there are recorded reasons (such as stoppage times) for explaining the gap between the actual performance and the required performance then, of course, these should be formulated into a 'Top loss' chart for the 'baseline' period (Figure 3.7).

There are many other statistical approaches for the analysis of data most notably control charts, box plots, correlation charts etc. For most situations, the simple time series plot and the top loss chart will be sufficient.

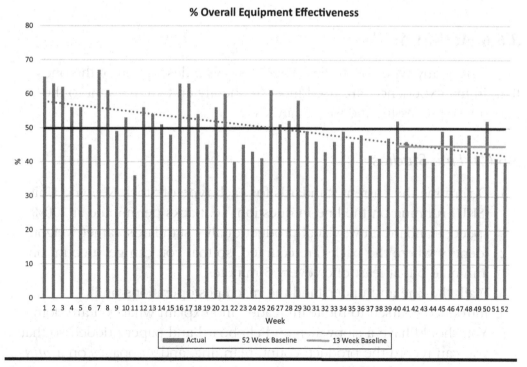

Figure 3.6   OEE time series chart.

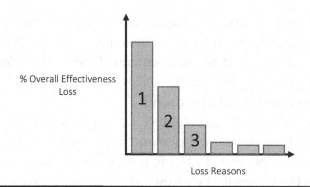

% Overall Effectiveness
Loss

Loss Reasons

Figure 3.7   Top loss chart.

It is important to not assume that the data are showing an accurate picture of the situation as its validity and consistency will not be known, particularly at the start of the analysis. However, through the interpolation of the baseline charts with your findings from subsequent studies and observations, you will be able to build the picture of the root causes of the current shortfall versus the expectations of the *Client.*

If the objective of the analysis is to reduce costs, a financial loss analysis will enable improvements to be pin pointed. This is described in more detail later in this section under cost benefits.

3.6.6 Activity Studies

There are many types of studies. There follows a description of the ones that, in my experience, are used most frequently and are relevant to the majority of processing industry analyses.

3.6.6.1 Line Studies

1. Determine the current standards for each type of Stock Keeping Unit (SKU) running on the line in question, i.e. packs per minute at 100% speed; standard crew; visual product quality standards; target weight.
2. Identify where the packs are counted, so that you can get a count once a minute but at least once every 5 minutes.
3. Walk the line and understand the machines/operations on it.
4. Introduce yourself to the team leader and explain what you are doing.
5. You should have a stopwatch and clipboard and paper gridded so that you can record the product; count, manning, and stoppages on a *minute-by-minute* basis plus any observations.

6. Following the study (usually more than one hour), you can produce charts such as those shown in Figures 3.8–3.10.
7. Earned minutes = packs produced/standard rate × standard crew.
8. Attended minutes = crew observed on the line × time period (this would be 1 if an observation was being made every minute).
9. Calculate the **overall equipment effectiveness** (OEE) for the study = sum of good packs/packs that would have been made at the standard rate × 100.
10. Calculate the productivity (or labour utilisation) for the study = sum of all earned minutes/total attended minutes × 100.
11. Review the data and make your conclusions.
12. Put your recommendations under the headings of People, Plant, Systems and Procedures.

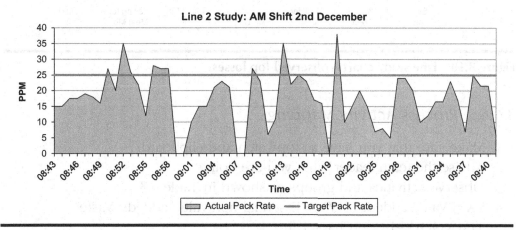

Figure 3.8   Line study chart: packs per minute.

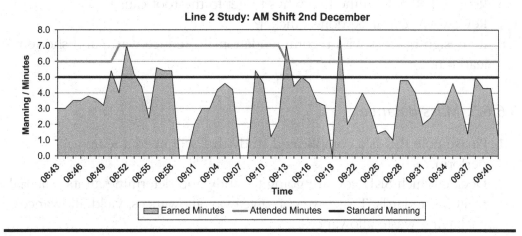

Figure 3.9   Line study chart – manning.

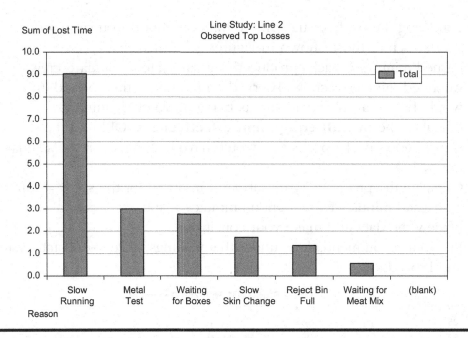

Figure 3.10 Line study chart – observed top losses.

3.6.6.2 *Process Activity Mapping*

1. Make sure that you have a stopwatch and clipboard.
2. Advise the team leader what you are doing.
3. Observe activities and groups as shown in Table 3.3.
4. VA = Value added; ENVA = Essential non-value added; Waste = TIMWOOD +1 (see Chapter 5).
5. Review waste with the 'five whys' to get to the root cause.
6. Review ENVA with the five whys to get to the root cause.
7. Review VA; can it be done quicker?
8. Re-design process with recommendations to reduce waste and shorten lead times.

3.6.6.3 *Mass Balance*

1. Please note this is a complicated study that will need a team to perform.
2. Decide which SKU you are going to study and determine all its material related standards: Target weight; giveaway allowances; yield allowances; packaging waste allowances.
3. Book the time for the study with production and planning management.

Table 3.3 Process Activity Study

Step	Description	Type	Time/s	Inventory	People	Machine	Notes	VA	ENVA	Waste
1	Pick packaging	Operation	120	10 cases	1	FLT	1000 per case		X	
2	Hold at bay	Delay	90	10 cases	0					X
3	Move to line	Movement	50/trip	5 cases/ trip	1	EPT	2 trips		X	X
4	Store at line		7200	10 cases	0					X
5	Use on line		1/pack	1 pack	6	Case packing line	Waste 2%	X		X
6	Hold at the end of line		10800	9800 packs	0		Waiting for movement to warehouse			X

4. Walk the area with a recipe and bill of materials and identify all the operations that will be used in the product manufacture, where material and packaging could be lost and any other points of interest.
5. Go somewhere quiet and plan it out:
   a. A clean bin is placed at each loss point.
   b. Documents to count product are prepared for each point.
   c. Who needs to be briefed and what they need to know.
   d. Arrange for a briefing time at least an hour before the start.
6. Brief the team and ensure bins and documents are in place.
7. Ensure that all raw materials and packaging for the run is fully weighed out and counted and separated from normal production.
8. Run the trial. Your role is to walk along the line and make sure that all losses are captured, documents are completed and points of interest are captured.
9. At the end of the trial, count the finished product; what is left of the raw materials and packaging; plus, all the waste streams including giveaway.
10. Produce a chart showing the use of the material and packaging. A simplified Mass Balance chart is shown in Figure 3.11. Floor waste may be split down further. A similar chart can be derived for packaging. Analyse each waste using the five whys and make your conclusions and recommendations under the headings of People, Plant, Systems and Procedures.
11. De-brief the team and thank them for their input.

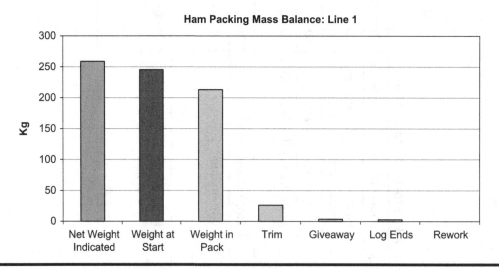

Figure 3.11   Mass balance chart.

3.6.6.4 Process Capability Studies

1. These can be performed on a variety of factors; the following is an illustration of how fill weight can be evaluated. In the very simple example shown below, it clearly shows that the filler is not capable of filling within the lower (425) and upper limits (435) (Figure 3.12).
2. To analyse further and calculate the process capability (CpK). Firstly derive the mean of all the readings – the easiest way is to enter each reading separately in a spreadsheet and divide the sum of all the reading results by the number of readings.
3. Then calculate the standard deviation, which is a measure of the variation. The simplest way is to use the STDEV function in Excel.
4. Then use this formula to calculate the CpK.

$$\text{CpK} = \big((\text{Upper Limit} - \text{Mean}) / (3 \times \text{Standard Deviation}) \big)$$

and

$$\big((\text{Mean} - \text{Lower Limit}) / (3 \times \text{Standard Deviation}) \big)$$

To be capable, each of the above numbers has to be greater than 1.33.
5. If the process is not capable, then highlight this in the analysis report as a priority area to resolve.

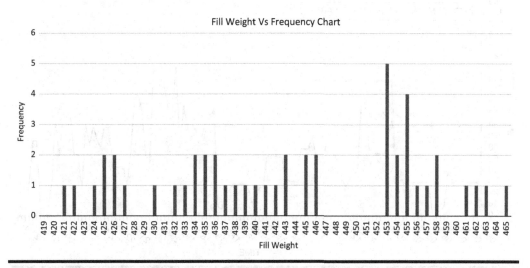

Figure 3.12 Fill weight versus frequency chart.

3.6.6.5 Demand versus Labour Resource Profile

1. Identify each type of value adding and essential non-value adding carried out in the area. And determine timings and manning for each: For a warehouse dealing in trolleys this list could look like Table 3.4.
2. Identify the manning on the period in question to determine the attended hours.
3. Count the activities by type and when they happen in the place of work (in time slots).
4. Develop a chart as shown on the following chart, which clearly shows the opportunity gap. This is done by multiplying the number of activities and cycle times per time slot.
5. Make your conclusions and recommendations under the headings of People, Plant, Systems and Procedures (Figure 3.13).

Table 3.4 Productivity Standards Recording

	Productivity Standards	
Activity	Cycle time per trolley (average of 10 studies)/minutes	Manning per cycle
Unload	0.59	1
Pick	1.79	1
Load	0.74	1

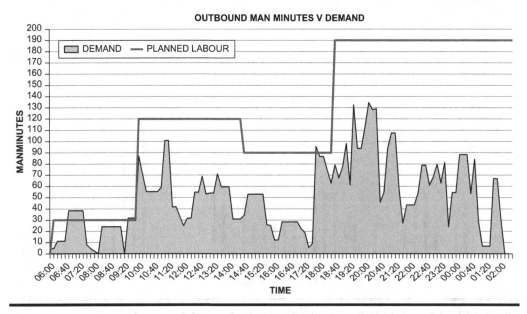

Figure 3.13 Demand versus labour chart.

3.6.6.6 Delay Ratio

1. Walk a prescribed route around the area in question at least 12 times. Each route should take at least 5 minutes to walk.
2. Each time someone comes into view, record what they are doing and categorise it.
3. Analyse the categories by graphing as shown: This is by frequency.
4. Categorise the activities into value added, essential non-value added and waste.
5. Make your conclusions and recommendations under the headings of People, Plant, Systems and Procedures (Figures 3.14 and 3.15).

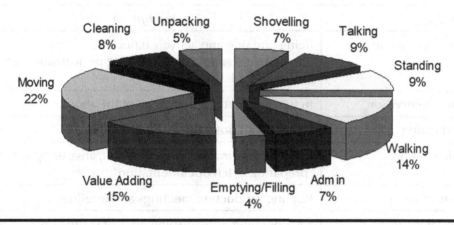

Figure 3.14   Delay ratio–activity pie chart.

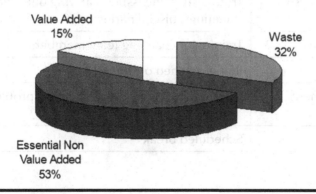

Figure 3.15   Delay ratio–value-added chart.

3.6.6.7 Day in the Life of Study

This procedure is used to assess how well the company is complying with best practice operational management practice.

1. Using the following categories, follow a manager around for a whole day/shift and record what they are doing on a minute-by-minute basis. Use the categories shown below.
2. Ask them why they are doing things and write down any pertinent comments.
3. Analyse the results into a pie chart and compare them to a best practice ideal that would have been derived before the study.
4. Make your conclusions and recommendations under the headings of People, Plant, Systems and Procedures (Table 3.5; Figures 3.16a and 3.16b).

Table 3.5   Day in the Life Study Time Categories

Work Type	Description
Active supervision	Being line side and actively (checking, asking, challenging, supporting) ensuring performance targets and standards are met
Passive supervision	In the area, but not doing any of the above
Coordinating	Liaising with boss/other departments
Administration	Entering information into computer, answering emails, preparing batch documentation
Routine meeting	Routine production meetings and briefings etc.
Undertaking team member's task	E.g. operating, replenishing lines or setting up
Troubleshooting issue	Troubleshooting issues, carrying out actions from meetings, disciplinaries
Developing team	Training or coaching team members
Developing self	Being coached or trained
Other improvement activity	Undertaking root cause structured problem solving
Break	Scheduled break

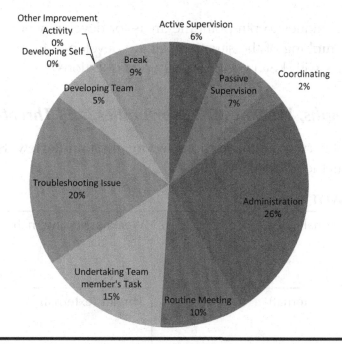

Figure 3.16a   Day in the life of study charts – actual.

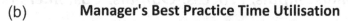

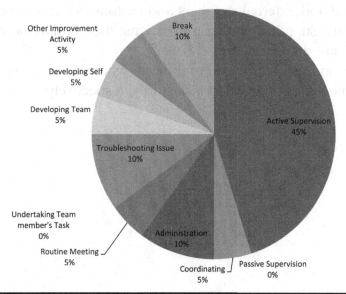

Figure 3.16b   Day in the life of study charts – best practice.

3.7 Organisation Review

Use these techniques to pin-point the areas for development and underpin your critical thinking of the situation. All are developed from observation and interviews with key people asking open questions.

3.7.1 Strengths, Weakness, Opportunities, and Threats (SWOT)

This is a summary of all the sections in Organisation Review. Build up a table that lists the following (Table 3.6).

Table 3.6   SWOT Table

Strengths (internal)	Weaknesses (internal)
Opportunities (external)	Threats (external)

3.7.2 Suppliers, Inputs, Process, Outputs, Customers (SIPOC)

Identify internal and external suppliers and customers to the process in question. Ask the suppliers and customers what their requirements are and how well they are doing? (Figure 3.17).

Red, amber and green are used to indicate where areas are not doing well, have some issues and done satisfactorily, respectively.

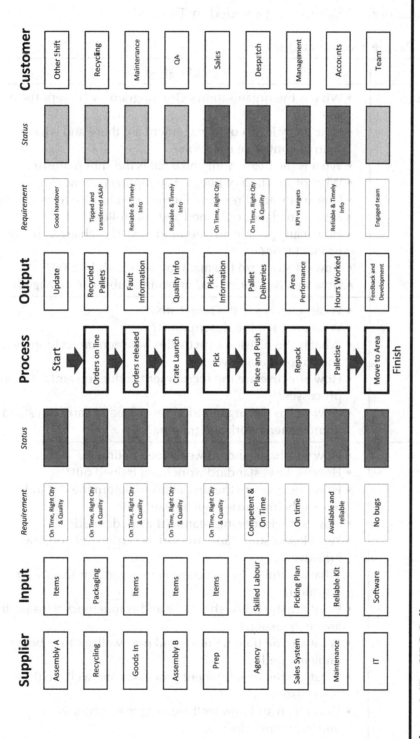

Figure 3.17 SIPOC diagram.

3.7.3 *People*

People evaluation questions are provided in Table 3.7.

Table 3.7   People Evaluation Questions

Area	Questions
Structures	• What is the organisation's Organogram – who reports to who? • How many levels of management are there and what is the span of control of each role? • What is the headcount and what is the shift pattern? • What proportion of people is temporary/agency? • How many are direct and indirect employees, respectively? • How is the labour planned and controlled? • How many people are required to staff each area/line by product type? • How effective are the manning standards by SKU? • How well is planned and unplanned absence managed?
Roles	• What roles are in the target area? • What are their job descriptions? • What is the division of activities between direct employees and support employees? • How effective are the recruitment, induction and retention processes? • How well is the organisation resourced to carry out standard, improvement work and training?
Skills	• How well has standard work been defined? • How well has standard work been trained out? • How effective are the processes to determine if standard work is being carried out as required? • How is the leadership standard work defined? • What leadership standard work is carried out and how effectively? • What are the skills and competency gaps for the area in question? • What are the leadership skills and competency gaps for the area in question? • What are the training plans and how well are they being implemented? • What are the development processes and well are these being used? • How much and how well are people involved in improvement activities?

(Continued)

Table 3.7 (Continued) People Evaluation Questions

Area	Questions
Communication	• What formal communication processes are used? • How effectively are the formal communication processes being used? • What types of informal communication processes were observed? • How well are informal communication processes used? • How visible is Leadership in the area?
Engagement	• How well do people identify with the espoused values of the company? • What are the morale levels in the target area/organisation as a whole? • How well do people identify with the aims of the company? • How well do people understand the strategy of the company and the part that they play in it? • What do people think about their managers? • How much do people agree with the statement 'This is a great place to work?' • What recognition processes are used and how effective are they?
Culture	• How would you describe the culture (e.g. 'command and control' or 'participative,' aggressive, or supportive, 'blame and shame' or 'support and learn')? • What 'stories' and 'symbols' are apparent? • What are the informal power structures? • How bureaucratic is the organisation? • How ethical is the organisation? • How root cause focused is the organisation, i.e. 'firefighting' or 'learn and improve?'

3.7.4 Facilities

Depending on the target area, some of the following questions will be relevant to the analysis (Table 3.8).

Table 3.8 Facilities Evaluation Questions

Area	Questions
Plant and machinery and areas	• What is the maintenance strategy? • How effective is the layout in terms of flow? • How capable are the processes? • What is the condition of the facilities? • What maintenance processes are used and how effectively? • How is the maintenance team organised and how effectively is it skilled and resourced? • What level of involvement do frontline teams have with regard to cleaning, inspection and lubrication routines? • What proportion of maintenance work is carried out in house? • How are spare parts managed? • How effective is the capital expenditure process (start to finish)?
Buildings and services	• What is the condition of the facilities? • How well do the buildings and areas comply with industry standards of good manufacturing practice? • Are regular surveys carried out as regards buildings' integrity? • What is the state of and how close to capacity are the various utilities systems such as gas, electricity, steam cooling gases and compressed air? • How effective are the heating, ventilation and air conditioning systems? • How is permitting organised and how effective is it?
IT	• What is the IT strategy? • What degree of alignment is there between the IT strategy and the plans of the rest of the organisation? • What type of enterprise resource planning (ERP) does the organisation use and what is the general view about how effective it is? • What gaps are observed between the IT infrastructure and industry's best practice? • How well are IT faults and issues supported and resolved by the internal IT team? • How effectively do IT systems support operational management and performance improvement? • What level of automation and Artificial Intelligence is used on site?

(Continued)

Table 3.8 (Continued)   Facilities Evaluation Questions

Area	Questions
Environmental	• What is the environmental strategy? • What degree of alignment is there between the environmental strategy and the plans of the rest of the organisation? • What condition and how effective are the drains and exhaust systems? • How well are environmental transmissions managed? • What energy-monitoring systems are in place? • What is the carbon footprint of the organisation and what plans are there to reduce this? • How compliant is the organisation with regard to keeping within legislative environmental requirements?
Site	• What are the traffic flow arrangements around the site? • How are deliveries and outbound transport managed at the site entrance and exit? • How well connected is the site to the road network? • How good are relationships with neighbours to the site? • Are there any limitations with regard to operating hours considering the location of the site and its proximity to neighbours? • What state of readiness is the site's major incident and disaster recovery plans (DRP)?

3.7.5 Lean Benchmark

In their ground-breaking book, *The Machine that Changed the World*, Womack, Jones and Roos (Simon and Schuster 1991) explained the evolution of lean manufacturing practices. 'Lean' is a pivotal Continuous Improvement philosophy espoused by companies such as Toyota.

Depending on the objectives of the analysis, it may be useful to undertake a review of where the organisation is on the 'Lean spectrum.' The following 'Lean Benchmark' can be used as a quick evaluation for a processing organisation. There are many more complicated versions, but this will give a reasonable overview of the current status. The following is an example from an analysis (Figure 3.18).

	Characteristic	Not Evident	Partly	Compliant	Comments
PLANT	Rapid changeover	1			Not witnessed
	Preventative Maintenance		1		PPM up to date but can fall behind owing to machine availability
	Excellent housekeeping			1	
	Operations are set close together with good flow			1	
	Low Inventory Levels	1			High levels of base material (weeks of cover)
PROCESS	Reject prevention through integrated quality control			1	Comprehensive
	Quality defects are displayed in the area	1			Not witnessed
	Standard operating procedures (SOP's) exist for all activities and are displayed at the operation.		1		Exist but not located at machines
	Visibility of Daily/Weekly production plan	1			None
	Visibility of attainment of Hourly performance/losses	1			No short interval control vs plan or targets
	Visibility of daily weekly performance/losses		1		DWOR report exists but is not user friendly to use/analyse. Efficiency and wastage figures not robust. Productivity not measured
	Visibility of bottleneck performance	1			Not witnessed
	Visibility of lead-times	1			
	Historical performance visibility		1		Board level trending. Visual trending of data on boards required
	Graphs of quality, delivery, productivity, cost reductions (improvement projects), and people (absence, health & safety)				
	Short Interval Control apparent	1			Not seen
	Defined Operational Management Process	1			6am meeting only
	Defined Strategy Deployment Process	1			Not seen
PEOPLE	First Line Managers are process and people managers	1			Competent and committed people whose performance could be improved through the adoption of structured processes
	Multi-skilled workers		1		Good technically but not with Continuous Improvement
	Skill flexibility of all team members displayed		1		Skills matrices exist but are not displayed
	Team working		1		Stong internal support. No formal work teams
	High level of team involvement in continuous improvement activities	1			Not witnessed
	People are aware of how their role links to the strategy of the organisation	1			Not witnessed

7   6
28%

Figure 3.18   Lean benchmark assessment. Source: Clive Turner.

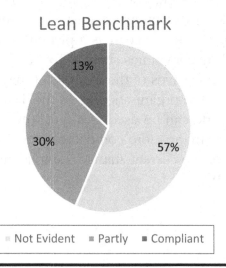

Lean Benchmark

13%

30%

57%

▪ Not Evident   ▪ Partly   ▪ Compliant

Figure 3.19   Lean benchmark chart.

Key:

- ■ PPM: Planned Preventative Maintenance.
- ■ DWOR: Daily Weekly Operating Report.
- ■ Short Interval Control: Shop floor visual performance management and review rituals that aim to highlight actual performance versus requirements shortfalls and address them immediately.
- ■ Operational Management Processes: A defined system for reviewing and managing daily operational performance (see Chapter 4).
- ■ Strategy Deployment Process: A defined system for identifying and delivering improvement activities that will enable the operational strategy to be delivered (see Chapter 6) (Figure 3.19).

3.8 Final Proposal Report

Typically, this would be a 'Powerpoint' presentation with each of the areas of the plan covered by relevant slides. The final slides in the presentation would cover the following areas:

3.8.1 Recommendations and Conclusions

In drawing together all the findings, it is important to link each relevant **Issue/Loss** observed with the **Evidence** gathered and the recommended **Countermeasures**. This can be presented in a 'Line-of-Sight' table (Table 3.9).

Table 3.9   Line-of-Sight Table

Issue/Loss	Evidence	Countermeasures
Long changeover times	• Last quarter downtime records indicated largest loss area, however, differing recording methods observed. • 3 changeover studies showed disorganised changeover. • No review of changeover performance observed with corrective actions.	A. Create defined changeover KPI and recording processes and train out. B. Implement single minute exchange of dies (SMED) project on top three product groups. C. Establish daily operational review process with visual management and defined terms of reference. Implement on shop floor.

The countermeasures can then, in turn, be linked to the likely improvements in an improvement action plan using the structure shown in Table 3.10.

Table 3.10   Improvement Action Plan Structure

Countermeasure	Where	When	Who	How Much
A, B, C	Packing Line 1	By June 21	Ops Manager	10% OEE improvement
D, E		By July 21	Team leader 1	3% OEE improvement
F		By Aug 21	Team leader 2	2% OEE improvement
Improvement Plan				15% OEE improvement

3.8.2 Cost–Benefit Model

Often, the improvement plan will be linked to a financial benefit. The process for how this is developed is illustrated in Figure 3.20.

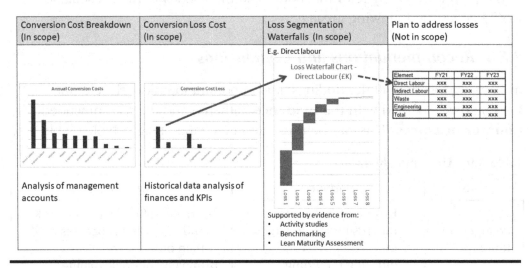

Figure 3.20   Conversion loss improvement process.

This example relates to the 'conversion costs' that a manufacturing unit incurs, i.e. not including the base material purchasing costs nor downstream logistics costs.

Steps:

1. Determine the demand levels and conversion costs by category for the current financial year.

2. Using a zero loss basis (e.g. 100% OEE, 100% Yield, zero breakdown etc.), determine what the conversion costs would have been and then calculate the losses for each area.
3. Use this information to pin point loss areas for improvement and focus as they relate back to the specific objective for the analysis.
4. From your investigations and using the improvement plan, calculate the financial benefit (using an appropriate financial rationale such as labour hours reduction) of each countermeasure and show the elements in a waterfall chart.
5. Summarise the annual benefits in a table for the next 3 financial years.

Please also refer to the cost–benefit model development for the improvement projects explained in Chapter 7.

3.9 Project Handover

Should the *Client* want to go onto the next stage and implement the project there will be handover to the team delivering the project.

The first stage will be to develop a project charter and milestone plan. How to do this is described in Chapter 7.

Effective communication at this point to the wider team is also extremely important **particularly** if the CI team is external (e.g. consultants)– notices, 'Town Hall' meetings, introducing who we are, why we are there, our experience and allaying fears about the 'strangers come to sack everyone.'

Chapter 4

Operational Management Facilitation

A ship can't be happy unless she's efficient and she certainly won't be efficient unless she's happy.

'In Which We Serve' (1942)

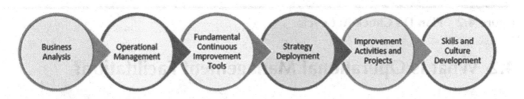

Figure 4.1 Operational Management.

4.1 Why Is Operational Management Facilitation Undertaken?

It's an often-repeated cliché that 'if you don't measure it you cannot improve it,' so from the point of view of Continuous Improvement, it is vital that performance is measured (shown in the second step of Figure 4.1). The 'Plan Do Check Act' (PDCA) cycle shown in Figure 4.2 is an iterative four-stage approach for improving processes, products or services and for resolving problems.

DOI: 10.4324/9781003244707-4

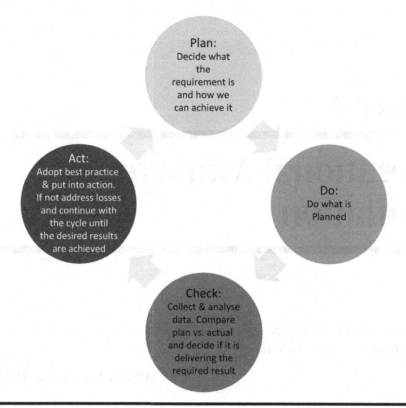

Figure 4.2 Plan Do Check Act cycle.

4.2 What Is Operational Management Facilitation?

The Operational Management PDCA Cycle is essentially a system that an organisation uses on a day-to-day basis as part of normal operations to ensure that it meets minimum performance requirements. In Chapter 2, I described this as 'Keep the trains running on time' and 'deliver our promises.'

To be effective and give a 'holistic' view of performance, an organisation can use the following areas in which to categorise its performance.

- ■ Safety
- ■ Quality
- ■ Delivery
- ■ Cost
- ■ Morale

Figure 4.3   The SQDCM 'Book shelf.'

If you imagine these areas on a bookshelf, Safety and Morale are the most important as they hold up the other areas and stop the operation 'falling over.' Also, in terms of reviewing them, you go from 'left to right,' i.e. Safety first, then Quality and so on (Figure 4.3).

Operational Management Facilitation is the six-step process that is followed to introduce and maintain the system within an organisation (Figure 4.4).

Figure 4.4   The six steps of Operations Management Facilitation.

4.3 When Is Operational Management Facilitation Undertaken?

Although it is shown in the figure above as a linear process with a start and finish, it is in reality an ongoing cycle of activities that is described in Section 4.6.4 ('Ensure Sustainability'). Within organisations without a Continuous Improvement culture, it is the 'first implementation step' of the Continuous Improvement journey as it forms the foundation from which all improvement activities are initiated and ultimately sustained.

4.4 Who Undertakes Operational Management Facilitation?

In the first instance, this is usually a Continuous Improvement Practitioner whose aim is to develop it with the Operations team and then to hand this process over to them.

4.5 How to Undertake Operational Management Facilitation?

4.5.1 Determine the KPI Structure

Ideally, this would be initiated on a strategic level by holding a workshop with the organisation's Senior Leadership team to determine the Key Performance Indicators (KPIs) and objectives of the organisation. Please refer to Sections 6.5.1–6.5.3 of Strategy Deployment in Chapter 6.

Often though, this is started by working with the local Senior Manager and her immediate team who will be able to identify safety quality delivery cost morale (SQDCM) KPIs that will enable them to manage their area more effectively.

For each of the SQDCM areas, create a 'KPI tree' and RACI (Responsible, Accountable, Consulted, Involved) matrix like that shown below. This example is for a quality priority (Figure 4.5).

Level 1 is Organisation level, Level 2 is Area/Process level, Level 3 is Machine/Activity level. With the team, identify KPIs for each level that are:

Relevant: They are *linked* to organisation's priorities. In this example, the team has identified the largest contributors to complaints at Level 2.

Meaningful: The people who are responsible for the measure both understand and 'own' them and the expected target.

Actionable: If the KPI is below target, the team who are reviewing the KPI must be able to take action to restore or improve it or escalate it if they are unable to resolve it.

Ensure that the full 'spread' of KPIs are covered, i.e. SQDCM but, to keep the focus, ensure there are as few as possible at each level. A good rule of thumb is no more than 15 SQDCM KPIs at Level 2.

Business Priority: Delight the Customer

Ref	Level 1	Level 2	Level 3	Link	R	A	C	I
1	Customer Complaints				Quality Manager	General Manager	Site Exec	Operations Director
2		Seal Failure Rate		1	Assembly Manager	Operations Manager	Operations, Quality, Engineering	Site Exec
3		Foreign Body Rate		1	Hygiene Manager	Quality Manager	Operations, Quality, Engineering	Site Exec
4			Pre-start Checks Confirmed	2	Line Leader	Shift Manager	Area Engineer, Quality Technician	Assembly Manager
5			GMP Audit Score	3	Hygiene Supervsior	Hygiene Manager	Line Leader, Shift Manager	Quality Manager

Figure 4.5   KPI tree and RACI.

4.5.2 *Identify the Review Structure*

Once you have identified the KPIs and the RACI matrix, a review (i.e. meeting and ritual) structure that links hourly, to shiftly, to daily, and to weekly intervals can be specified. It is important that:

■ It is developed with the team. This can be one to one or in a team 'workshop' session.
■ There is a review by a relevant team for each time segment and/or level (Figure 4.6).

Think gears linking together – each meeting or ritual is a gear which needs to be operating effectively for whole machine to run effectively!

■ Responsibility and action are owned and carried out at the relevant level of the organisation.
■ The why, what, how, when, where and who are identified for each review.

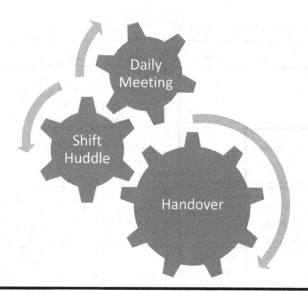

Figure 4.6　Review structure.

- There are review processes where the quality of the reviews is managed.
- A 'rich picture' or 'cascade' is constructed to help gain agreement **and communicate** (Figure 4.7).

Figure 4.7   Operational Management System rich picture.

4.6 Common Review Meetings and Rituals

Common Review Meetings and Rituals are provided in Table 4.1.

Table 4.1   Common Review Meetings and Rituals

Time Interval	Review or Ritual	Visual Management	Purpose
Now	Escalation (ESC)	Andon light or cable Escalation sheet	Immediately flag a variance of performance or standard versus a trigger condition
Hourly	Short Interval Control (SIC)	Line side board or screen	Review of actual versus target results by Team Leader and actions required
Mid Shift	Managing By Walking Around (MBWA)	Line side Boards SQDCM Boards	Area Leader confirmation that standards and performance is on track
Shift	Shift Handover (SHO)	Line Side Boards Shift Handover Log	Ensure smooth transfer between shifts of all vital information including issues by Operators and Area Leaders
Day	Scheduling Meeting (SCM)	Planning Board	Agreement of tomorrow's schedule and review of today's progress
Day	Daily Area Review (DAR)	SQDCM Boards Daily Weekly Operating Report	Area Leader confirmation that standards and performance is on track
Day	Daily Operations Review (DOR)	Daily Weekly Operating Report	Operations Manager confirmation that standards and performance is on track
Week	Weekly Operations Review (WOR)	Bowler reports and/or time series charts showing performance versus target. Top loss reports Basic Problem Solving Tracker Sustainability Tracker	Site Leader confirmation that standards and performance is on track

(Continued)

Table 4.1 (Continued) Common Review Meetings and Rituals

Time Interval	Review or Ritual	Visual Management	Purpose
Week	Continuous Improvement Review (CIR)	QUAD reports showing progress of CI projects Projects Board Strategy Deployment Board	Site Leader confirmation that standards and performance is on track
Week	Planning Meeting (PLM)	Plans for each resource	Common agreement on the plan for the coming weeks to ensure all resources are in place
Week	Engineering Priorities (ENP)	Agreed Schedule Board or list	Agreement of priority maintenance work
Month	Monthly Operations Review (MOR)	Bowler reports and/or time series charts showing performance versus target Strategy Deployment Board	Senior Leader Confirmation that Operations Strategy is on track

4.6.1 Create Terms of Reference

A review or 'ritual' is *Standard Work* that needs to be carried out according to a clearly defined procedure (Figure 4.8). Compliance with the standards will create the 'drumbeat' for the department and in turn the organisation. The terms of Reference should be created with the team for each review identified in Section 4.5.2 that sets out:

Figure 4.8 'Keeping the beat.'

DAILY OPERATIONS REVIEW TOR

DURATION: 30 Minutes (max) **FREQUENCY:** Daily 09:00am **LOCATION:** Shop Floor Meeting Area	**ATTENDEES:** Dept Managers or deputies Chair to revolve Meeting coach to revolve

OBJECTIVE: TO MAKE TODAY BETTER THAN YESTERDAY

- To review yesterday's performance of the Site and Production Areas and address any Escalations
- To review performance vs. targets and trends
- To identify and action any events that may impact upon operational performance.
- To ensure that the top losses are identified and ownership is assigned.
- To identify further improvement opportunities.
- To agree priorities for today

AGENDA: (mins)

- Action Log Review..5
- Review of dashboard by Exception and Escalations..15
- Subject of the day (H&S etc.).......................3
- Recognition of good performance.................2
- Priorities and AOB......................................5

INPUTS	**OUTPUTS**
• DWOR Dashboard (completed) • Escalations from Daily Area Meetings • Action Log	• Agree priorities for today • Updated action log • Cascade escalation support and recognition

GROUND RULES

- Meeting should be 'snappy', action orientated and last no more then 30 minutes. No interruptions.
- Attendance is compulsory; send a deputy if you cannot attend. Phones on silent.
- Be on time, the meeting will not wait for you.
- Ensure you set realistic timescales for action points and you complete them within your set timescales
- Be prepared;
    - Understand key issues & root cause before the meeting
    - problem solving before the meeting

Figure 4.9   Example of a terms of reference.

An example of Terms of Reference is given in Figure 4.9.

- ■ Attendees
- ■ Agenda
- ■ Objectives
- ■ Inputs and outputs
- ■ Duration
- ■ Frequency
- ■ Ground rules
- ■ Accountabilities (Figure 4.9)

4.6.2 *Build Visual Management*

Visual Management (VM) for each review should include trend charts versus targets, action logs and any other relevant data and facts that support the effective running of the operation. It should follow these principles (Figure 4.10).

Figure 4.10   Develop it with the team. Source: Riverford Organic Farmers –
'Keeping the beet.'

- A shop floor-based SQDCM Board is the heart of the Operational Management System.
- Visible from a minimum of 10 m.
- Easy to see if we are 'having a good day' – shows where the issues are and what action is taken.
- Figure 4.11: Each section of the board can be headed with one of the SQDCM letters that are then coloured in red or green by the team on a

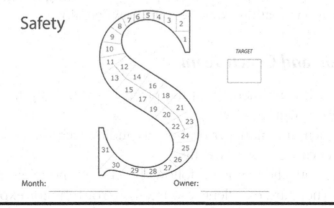

Figure 4.11   SQDCM letters.

Figure 4.12   SQDCM board. Source: Riverford Organic Farmers – 'Keeping the beet.'

daily basis depending if the primary KPI in that category was above or below target for the date in question.

■ All KPIs can be presented using A3-sized templates – use red and green dry wipe pens as opposed to print outs (Figure 4.12).

■ Each of the KPIs shows performance versus target (Figures 4.13 and 4.14).

■ Do not forget the 'power of the pen' – by writing things up to share information creating awareness and ownership.

4.6.3 *Train and Coach Teams*

■ Train each team member at the place of work using the Terms of Reference (Figure 4.15).

■ Train each line manager on how to audit/coach the process to ensure it is being carried out correctly.

■ Engage with the team and follow the GROW model at the place of work. There are excellent resources on YouTube for explaining how to use the Grow model (Figure 4.16).

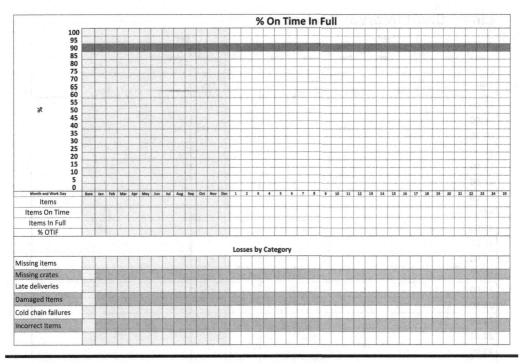

Figure 4.13   Example of A3 template of a 'Delivery' KPI.

- Develop 'health checks' that enable reviews to be assessed and coached in a consistent manner (Figure 4.17).
- Develop a coaching rota, involving all of the ritual or review meeting participants and ensure that all reviews are regularly coached, trended and improvements actioned (Figure 4.18).

If you learn either to drive or a musical instrument or a new sport, it is expected that you will have to 'put the practice in' to get better and become competent. It is my experience that this does not often translate to the workplace, particularly concerning new management processes. If something seems difficult at first, it will often get dropped if management do not show an interest and support it. Let's be clear, Operational Management Systems are 'hard work' at the start and the team may/will see them as additional effort that they just do not have time for given all the issues they have to sort out. It is often difficult for them to see the very fact that they do not have an effective review process is the root cause of why there are so many issues. It is crucial therefore that teams practice all of the rituals on a daily basis until it becomes embedded in their 'muscle memory' and they could not imagine not doing them as the benefits are so obvious. This 'acting your

Line 1 Short Interval Control

			Operator:						Date:
TIME	Safety	Quality Compliance	GMP	Plan	Actual	OEE	Downtime	Line Waste	COMMENTS
Target	All hazards identified & resolved?	All line checks ok?	GMP ok?			60%	0 Mins	<1Kg	
07:00									
08:00									
09:00									
10:00									
11:00									
12:00									
13:00									
14:00									
15:00									
16:00									
17:00									
18:00									
19:00									
20:00									
21:00									
22:00									
23:00									
00:00									
01:00									
02:00									
03:00									
04:00									
05:00									
06:00									
Total									

Change Over Performance

Product 1	Product 2	Plan	Actual	%	COMMENTS
Total					

Figure 4.14   Example of a line board for hourly 'Short Interval Control.'

Ritual/Method	Name 1	Name 2	Name 3	Name 4	Name 5	Name 6	Name 7	Name 8	Name 9	Name 10	Name 11	Name 12	Name 13
Data Capture	Y	Y	Y	Y	Y		Y	Y	Y	Y			
Operations Management Process Development	Y	Y	Y										
Short Interval Control	Y	Y	Y	Y	Y		Y	Y	Y	Y	Y	Y	Y
Engineering Priorities Meeting	Y	Y		Y	Y								
MBWA	Y	Y	Y	Y			Y	Y	Y	Y			
Daily Area Meeting	Y	Y	Y	Y	Y		Y	Y	Y	Y			
Weekly Operations Review	Y	Y	Y										
Weekly SLT Review	Y	Y											
Productivity Review													
Monthly Operations Review	Y												
Data and Facts Analysis	Y	Y	Y										
Lean Fundamentals	Y	Y	Y	Y			Y				Y	Y	Y
Lean Project Management Fundamentals													
Root Cause Behaviours													
Basic Problem Solving	Y	Y	Y	Y			Y	Y	Y	Y	Y	Y	Y
Sustainability Auditing	Y	Y								Y			

Figure 4.15   Set up a training matrix to show who needs to be trained with what.

Figure 4.16   The GROW model for coaching.

way into a new way of thinking' methodology has close links with psycho-logical therapy techniques (see Chapter 8).

If you build it they will come!

For each meeting or ritual, appoint a coach and ask them to give feedback to the team on how it went at the end. The 'health check' can provide a basis for this coaching. The score is not the important aspect, it is getting the team to talk and reflect on their own behaviours and commit to making improvements that is the point; just like a golf coach giving you guidance

Daily Area Meeting Health Check					Scoring:	
					1	Requirement met
Team:	Assessor:		Date:		0	Did not meet requirement

No.	Observation Requirements	Score	Assessment YES	NO	Comments
1	All SQDCM KPIs are covered, the Area/Board room conforms to the company standard and is neat and tidy.				
2	KPIs have been updated by those responsible for them using the correct colour dry wipe pens, allowing the team to clearly understand the performance of the area.				
3	The owners of the KPIs understand trends and losses. They bring evidence to the review backed up with data and facts.				
4	A Terms of Reference is visible and is followed. There is full attendance				
5	Team members stand at the board and report their performance and if required they write up their own actions on the board				
6	There are minimal late actions				
7	Meeting atmosphere is productive & effective: all those present contribute to the meeting with constructive questions and challenges.				
8	Any 'red' has an action or every participant agrees the action is already carried out				
9	Actions address the root cause of issues				
10	High performance or contributions are recognised.				
11	Basic Problem Solving activities are triggered, reviewed and closed out				
	Total				
	% Compliance				

Figure 4.17   Health check template.

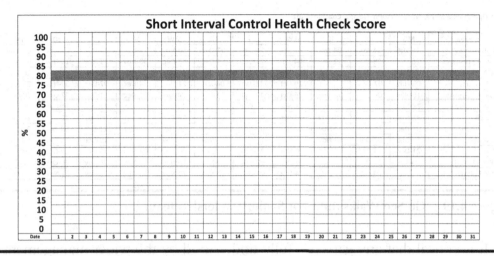

Figure 4.18   Short interval control daily tracker.

and feedback on your swing immediately before and after you have hit the ball, respectively.

To reinforce the 'what gets measured gets done' message, it is often useful to track the progress of the various rituals on the SQDCM Board (Figure 4.18).

4.6.4 Ensure Sustainability

To sustain a sustainable CI culture, it is essential that Senior Leadership own and drive the process forward.

There are two key requirements: Leadership Engagement ('Go See Walks') and a Structured Sustainability Audit programme that produces an 'audit score,' which is typically reviewed at a Weekly Operations Review.

The Senior Leadership team is responsible for facilitating the delivery of this element and its ongoing sustainability.

4.7 'Go See Walks Rota'

Senior Leadership being seen on the shop floor and visibly confirming with the teams that the CI Process is happening to standard is crucial. This embeds the CI culture.

'Coaching' the operational ritual (SIC, MBWA, Daily Area Meetings etc.) standards is a structured way of doing this that can be monitored at a Weekly Operations Review (Figure 4.19).

SLT Operational Management System 'Go See' Coaching Rota

Area	MG	JO	IS	EW	KV	LD	MW	SO	VD	RD	IM
SIC Preserves	19-Oct	11-Jan	04-Jan	21-Dec	14-Dec	07-Dec	30-Nov	23-Nov	16-Nov	09-Nov	02-Nov
MBWA Preserves	26-Oct	19-Oct	11-Jan	04-Jan	21-Dec	14-Dec	07-Dec	30-Nov	23-Nov	16-Nov	09-Nov
DAM Preserves	02-Nov	26-Oct	19-Oct	11-Jan	04-Jan	21-Dec	14-Dec	07-Dec	30-Nov	23-Nov	16-Nov
SIC Desserts	09-Nov	02-Nov	26-Oct	19-Oct	11-Jan	04-Jan	21-Dec	14-Dec	07-Dec	30-Nov	23-Nov
MBWA Desserts	16-Nov	09-Nov	02-Nov	26-Oct	19-Oct	11-Jan	04-Jan	21-Dec	14-Dec	07-Dec	30-Nov
DAM Desserts	23-Nov	16-Nov	09-Nov	02-Nov	26-Oct	19-Oct	11-Jan	04-Jan	21-Dec	14-Dec	07-Dec
SIC B2B	30-Nov	23-Nov	16-Nov	09-Nov	02-Nov	26-Oct	19-Oct	11-Jan	04-Jan	21-Dec	14-Dec
MBWA B2B	07-Dec	30-Nov	23-Nov	16-Nov	09-Nov	02-Nov	26-Oct	19-Oct	11-Jan	04-Jan	21-Dec
DAM B2B	14-Dec	07-Dec	30-Nov	23-Nov	16-Nov	09-Nov	02-Nov	26-Oct	19-Oct	11-Jan	04-Jan
SIC FL4SH	21-Dec	14-Dec	07-Dec	30-Nov	23-Nov	16-Nov	09-Nov	02-Nov	26-Oct	19-Oct	11-Jan
MBWA FL4SH	04-Jan	21-Dec	14-Dec	07-Dec	30-Nov	23-Nov	16-Nov	09-Nov	02-Nov	26-Oct	19-Oct
DAM FL4SH	11-Jan	04-Jan	21-Dec	14-Dec	07-Dec	30-Nov	23-Nov	16-Nov	09-Nov	02-Nov	26-Oct

Figure 4.19   'Go See Walks Rota' for Senior Leadership team.

It is critical that any gaps are fully understood by the wider management team and that there is a coherent action plan to address these.

4.8 Sustainability Audit

In order to ensure that Operational Management processes are sustained, it is not only important to measure the performance improvement being targeted (i.e. the KPI) but also to measure, and make apparent to all, the change in behaviour. This is essential if we want to ensure that the change is sustained and becomes an integral part of a sustainable Continuous Improvement culture. We can do this by using a Sustainability Audit process.

Step 1: Create a table that highlights all the reviews that have been identified within the Operational Management System (Figure 4.20).

Operational Management Sustainability Audit						Maturity Score	0%	Sustainability Score	0%
						Target	90%	Target	90%
Process Owner:							Comments/Next Steps		
Method Operational Management	Target	OK?	Standard	Trained	Used				
Short Interval Control	8								
Engineering Priorities Meeting	8								
Managing By Walking Around	8								
Daily Area Meeting	8								
Daily Operations Review	8								
Weekly Department Operations Review	8								
Weekly Site Operations Review	8								
Basic Problem Solving	8								

Figure 4.20   Sustainability audit.

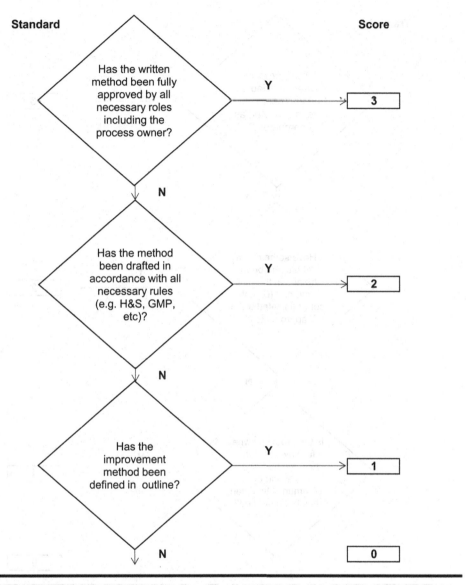

Figure 4.21   Standard decision tree.

Step 2: On a regular basis, review the progress of each method using the
following 'decision trees' (Figures 4.21–4.23).

It is good practice to use the results of the Health Checks to inform whether
a review or ritual is being used effectively as this encourages the daily practice that is so crucial during the early stages of a Continuous Improvement
implementation.

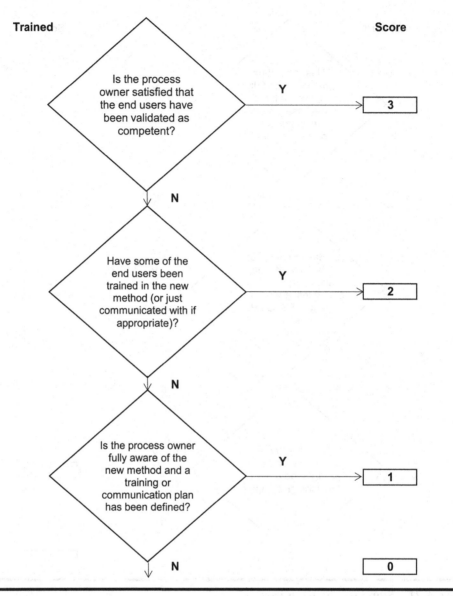

Figure 4.22   Trained decision tree.

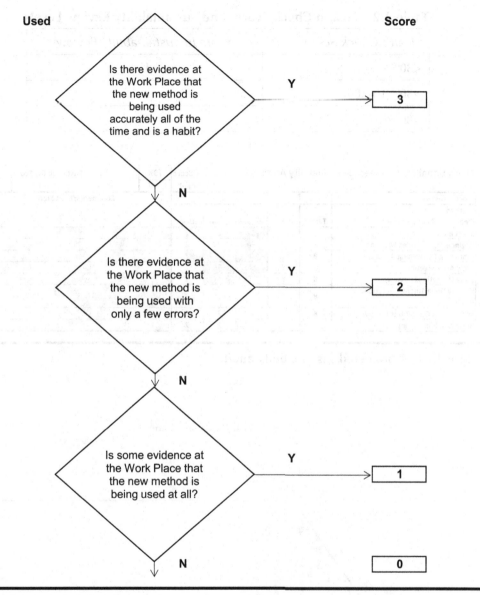

Figure 4.23 Used decision tree.

Table 4.2 Health Check Scores and Sustainability Review Levels

Health Check Score	Score in Sustainability Review
<30%	1
>30% to <80%	2
>80%	3

Operational Management Sustainability Audit						Maturity Score	79%	Sustainability Score	38%
						Target	90%	Target	90%

Process Owner:						Comments/Next Steps
Method **Operational Management**	Target	OK?	Standard	Trained	Used	
Short Interval Control	8		3	2	2	
Engineering Priorities Meeting	8		3	2	2	
Managing By Walking Around	8	Y	3	3	3	
Daily Area Meeting	8	Y	3	3	2	
Daily Operations Review	8	Y	3	3	2	
Weekly Department Operations Review	8		2	2	2	
Weekly Site Operations Review	8		2	2	2	
Basic Problem Solving	8		2	2	2	

Figure 4.24 Completed sustainability audit.

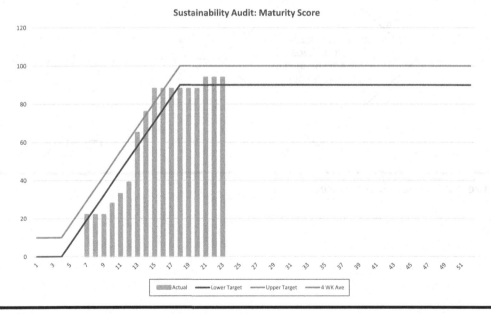

Figure 4.25 Weekly reporting of sustainability score.

It is recommended that a daily log of the Health Check scores is maintained for at least 6 months and the average of the score used with the Sustainability Review (Table 4.2).

After this period, the log frequency can be reduced to a weekly 'check-up,' with the frequency being increased if there is evidence of slippage. The 'Go See Walks' by senior leaders will help reinforce the message and ensure that standards are maintained.

The standard you walk past is the standard you accept!

Step 3: Update the table and then plot the score on a tracker to review progress (Figure 4.24).

The Maturity Score is the sum of all the Scores divided by the number of methods × 9.

The Sustainability Score is the number of methods that are greater than 8, i.e. 'strength in depth' and a 'habit' (Figure 4.25).

Using this methodology, both the installation and the sustainability period can be kept under review. It is really important to keep up the momentum and have a disciplined approach.

Chapter 5

Fundamental Continuous Improvement Tools

'If it ain't broke, don't fix it' is the slogan of the complacent, the arrogant or the scared. It's an excuse for inaction, a call to non-arms.

Colin Powell

Figure 5.1   Fundamental Continuous Improvement Tools.

5.1 Data Capture Systems

Effective Operational Management and Continuous Improvement (CI) of performance rely on the accurate collection of data to both determine the level of performance versus a target and, if there is a gap, what the reasons for this are. These results play a critical input in operational reviews (Figure 5.1).

For data collection to be effective, the data must be:

- Relevant: A measure linked to the business' Safety, Quality, Delivery, Cost, Morale priorities.
- Meaningful: Understood by the people who fill the data in and have to respond to it.

DOI: 10.4324/9781003244707-5

Table 5.1 Examples of Variable and Attribute Data

Variable Data Examples	Attribute Data Examples
%	Colour
Weight	Defect type
Length	Downtime type
Temperature	Good or bad
Viscosity	Correct or incorrect
Etc.	Etc.

■ Actionable: If the data amount is below expectation, it should prompt an action, i.e. the link between cause and effect should be clear.
■ Valid: Data should measure what it is supposed to measure.
■ Reliable: Different people collecting the same data should come up with the same results.
■ Easy to understand.
■ Trained out and checked/coached at regular intervals to assure quality.
■ As simple as possible to collect.
■ Visual – to drive the right behaviours.

There are two main types of data: Variable (or Continuous) data and Attribute data. The former is usually expressed as an amount or percentage, the latter by a count or a description (Table 5.1).

Attribute data can be expressed in a variable data format by adding up and expressing it as a percentage.

E.g. % Right First Time (a Quality Key Performance Indicator)

$$= \frac{\left(\text{No. Products in Total} - \text{No. Defective Products}\right) \times 100}{\text{No. Products in Total}}$$

Data collection formats can be manual or automatic or a combination of the two.

■ Manual: Data capture sheets that are completed by operators.
■ Automatic data capture: For example, check weighers, temperature recorders, transducers, sensors, error messages on the system, pick counts, etc. that then get interpreted by a computer programme.

In terms of what output is required, there needs to be a clear definition of the key performance indicator and how and where it is to be presented. This can be summarised in a data collection plan such as that shown below.

5.1.1 Data Collection Plan

This is an example of data capture plans for %Overall Equipment Effectiveness (OEE) and stoppage times (Table 5.2).

This plan will then need to be implemented by creating the elements of the data capture plan and then this should be trained out to the relevant responsible personnel.

There is an understandable temptation to rely on automatic data capture and reports generation. There are many business intelligence tools that provide ease of data capture and produce seemingly powerful reports that enable data to be 'cut and diced' in various ways. In my experience, the benefits of these systems are, in fact, illusory. What is gained in the slickness of the graphical reporting is more than made up by the losses of ownership and shop floor visibility of shop floor reporting that automatic systems seem to cause. The mantra is, keep it simple!

For example, consider the following chart for the presentation on safety quality delivery cost morale (SQDCM) board of all the data required to both manage the operation on day-to-day and month-to-month basis plus provide loss data that will enable improvements to be pinpointed. This shows the position on 5th April; the target is less than 10% downtime (Figure 5.2).

Table 5.2 Data Collection Plan

What	Type	How Measured	Related Conditions	Sampling Strategy	Where Recorded	Where Reported	Who
% Overall equipment effectiveness (% OEE)	Variable	No. Good products made in the available time/No. of good products that could have been at 100% filling rate in the available time expressed as percentage	Counts of good products made each hour	Count readout from checkweigher each hour	Data collection sheets	OEE recorded on line boards each hour (actual vs target)	Operator
			Shift Start and finish times		Data input sheet on Daily Weekly Operating Report	OEE on time series plot on SQDCM boards at end of shift	Team Leader
						Daily report of OEE by line by shift	Team Leader

(Continued)

Table 5.2 (Continued)   Data Collection Plan

What	Type	How Measured	Related Conditions	Sampling Strategy	Where Recorded	Where Reported	Who
Stoppage times	Attribute	Minutes by downtime type	• Changeover • Breakdowns • Waiting for raw material • Waiting for staff • Waiting for packaging • Line crash • Downstream failures • Cleaning	Each occurrence – start to finish of downtime	Data Collection sheet	Down time (DT) min recorded on line boards each hour	Operator
						DT min on loss chart on SQDCM boards at end of shift	Team Leader
					Data input sheet on Daily Weekly Operating Report	Daily report of DT min by type by line by shift	Team Leader

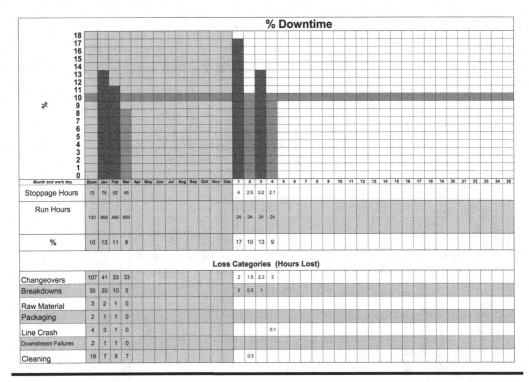

% Downtime

Month and work day	Base	Jan	Feb	Mar	Apr	May	Jun	Jul	Aug	Sep	Oct	Nov	Dec	1	2	3	4	5	6	7	8	9	10	11	12	13	14	15	16	17	18	19	20	21	22	23	24	25
Stoppage Hours	12	75	52	45										4	2.5	3.2	2.1																					
Run Hours	120	600	480	600										24	24	24	24																					
%	10	13	11	8										17	10	13	9																					

Loss Categories (Hours Lost)

	Base	Jan	Feb	Mar	Apr	May	Jun	Jul	Aug	Sep	Oct	Nov	Dec	1	2	3	4	5	6	7	8	9	10	11	12	13	14	15	16	17	18	19	20	21	22	23	24	25
Changeovers	107	41	33	33										2	1.5	2.2	2																					
Breakdowns	35	20	10	5										2	0.5	1																						
Raw Material	3	2	1	0																																		
Packaging	2	1	1	0																																		
Line Crash	4	3	1	0												0.1																						
Downstream Failures	2	1	1	0																																		
Cleaning	19	7	5	7										0.5																								

Figure 5.2   Downtime chart example.

5.2 The Continuous Improvement Plan

When I first became a Factory Operations Manager, I did not have a background in production management. I was for all intents and purposes 'dropped in the deep end' (my choice!). My boss at the time asked me, when I started in my new role, what my plan was. I thought: 'doesn't he realise that I am struggling to stay afloat at the moment, there is so much basic stuff to learn before I even come up with a plan!.' He kept repeating it until it finally dawned on me what he was asking me to do:

■ Evaluate how well the operation is performing now.
■ Determine where we needed to be and by when.
■ Come up with a plan to get there.
■ Tell him what my plan was!

For each of these four bullet points, I wrote down what I knew and discussed it with him – within 30 minutes I had a 'plan.' Over the coming weeks, we worked on it together with my team and came up with an agreed way forward which was reviewed and adjusted on a regular basis. In many ways, this simple process is at the heart of Continuous Improvement:

■ Having an improvement plan is an essential part of managing an operation and not a 'bolt on.'
■ It is something that can be arrived at very quickly. The main point I learned was 'not to let perfect get in the way of better!'

As we have learned, all operational performance can be affinitised under the SQDCM headings. A CI plan has the following basic structure (Table 5.3).

Table 5.3   Continuous Improvement Plan Structure

Area	What (KPIs) Examples	How (Counter-measure)	Where (Plant, Dept, Line etc.)	When (Due Date)	Who (Responsible for Delivery)	How Much (to Improve the KPI from x to y)
Safety	Total Injury Frequency Rate No. Accidents					
Quality	% Right First-Time Complaints per million units					
Delivery	Plan% On Time in Full % Overall equipment effectiveness					
Cost	Units per man hour % Yield £ Cost/Unit					
Morale	% Attendance % CI Sustainability 'Pulse' survey					

To get started, the '**How**' activities for a CI plan could be **Identified** through a combination of the following:

- Undertaking a Business Analysis (see Chapter 3).
- A brainstorming session with the local team using the question 'What are our issues that are hampering our SQDCM performance?' (see later in this section).
- Through the 'top losses' identified through the data capture system (see earlier).
- Undertaking a '7+1' waste review (see later in this section).
- Through a Detailed Process Mapping review (see later in this section).
- Undertaking a Voice of the Customer exercise (see later in this section).
- Undertaking a Value Stream Mapping exercise (see Chapter 7).

Then the potential activities can be **Prioritised** using an Impact and Effort matrix (see later in this chapter under Section 5.10).

Next, depending on the complexity of the problem, these can be **Assigned** to individuals and teams to **Deliver** and **Monitor** progress through a regular CI meeting. It is useful to remember the acronym IPAD-M:

IDENTIFY
PRIORITISE
ASSIGN
DELIVER
MONITOR

It is also useful to think of the whole process as an 'improvement engine.' Figure 5.3 shows this represented by a jet engine.

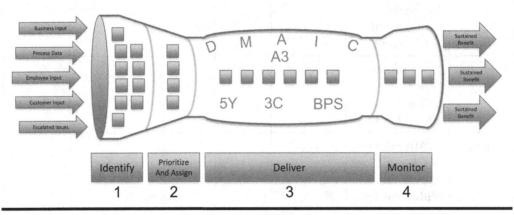

Figure 5.3   Improvement engine. Source: Grant Beverley.

This process is covered in more detail in Chapter 7 where we will go into the monitoring and governance process in more depth and explain the more complicated forms of problem-solving techniques. For now, remember, plan for success:

PLAN

Plan the work, work the plan

SUCCESS

The recipe for success:
Have a good story
Tell it well
Deliver it

Tom Von Weymarn

5.3 Brainstorming

Gather a group of people who are familiar with the area where the problem is occurring. Ideally, this will include the frontline team and the internal customers. Using 'post-its,' go around the team asking for ideas to be written down on the 'post-its' which are then placed on a flip chart. The team could be asked for problems or causes. The following rules should apply:

- No criticism or debate.
- Quantity over quality.
- Build on existing ideas.
- Freewheel – no idea is stupid.
- Round robin – say "pass" if a person does not have an idea this time around.
- Record all ideas.
- 'Sleep on it' if possible before the final evaluation.

When the ideas have dried up, the team is then asked to group them into common areas ('affinitise'), such as the 4Ms, on a flip chart (Figure 5.4).

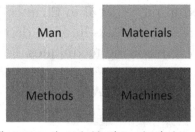

The team can then prioritise them using the Impact
and Effort matrix (section 5.10).

Figure 5.4   Affinitise and evaluation 4Ms matrix.

5.4 Data and Facts: Identifying Top Losses and Opportunities

Continuous Improvement relies on knowing the reason between where you want to be ('Target Result') and the current situation ('Actual Result'). This should always be based on data and facts and not 'opinion.'

5.4.1 Operational Gap

Consider the weekly result below for the OEE for Line A. There is an operational gap ('Gap 1') between the current target and the actual.

At the meeting where this key performance indicator (KPI) is reviewed (e.g. Weekly Operations Review), the team will want to hear from you about the root cause reasons for this gap, what you have done to close it and the support you require (Figure 5.5).

From the loss data that has been recorded on the data capture system or by other means, it is important to prepare an explanation for each of the loss areas. This is best presented as a 'Pareto Top Loss chart' (Figure 5.6).

Go to the meeting with annotations on the loss chart to show that you have understood the root causes of at least the three 'top losses,' have put actions in place to address these plus what support and/or further actions are required to make sure this current week is above target. This behaviour should be the same for any performance review meeting or ritual: e.g. Short Interval Control, Managing by Walking around Daily Area Meeting, Daily Operations review (Figure 5.7).

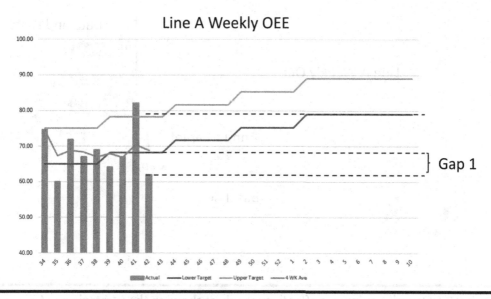

Figure 5.5   Overall equipment effectiveness chart showing the 'operational gap.'

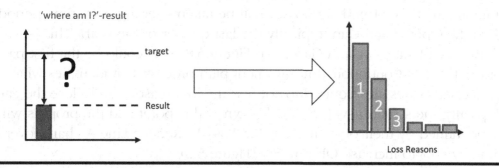

Figure 5.6   Analysis of the gap.

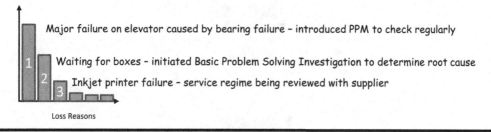

Figure 5.7   Detailed analysis of the gap.

5.4.2 Strategic Gap

The Operations Review meeting attendees will also want to know the 'data and facts' reasons for the gap between the current actual trend and the

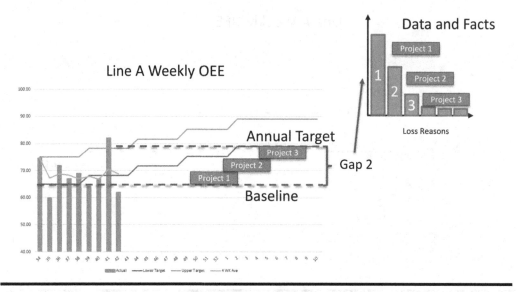

Figure 5.8 Overall equipment effectiveness chart showing the 'strategic gap.'

annual target. The trend and losses will be taken over a greater time period than the Operational Gap (typically the last quarter of the year). This is shown as a Strategic Gap ('Gap 2') in Figure 5.8. This could be the first part of the IPAD-M Continuous Improvement plan process as it identifies what projects/activities are required to address the loss reasons and 'close the gap.' Typically, the solutions will not be known at this point and the projects will be identified by their objective, e.g. for 'Loss 1': 'Reduce Line A changeover time by 30% to increase OEE by 5%' (Figure 5.8).

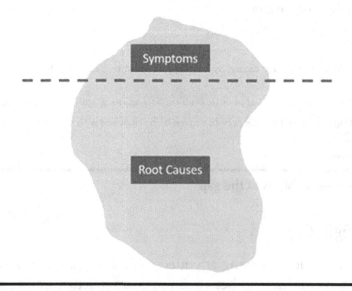

Figure 5.9 Iceberg model of questioning.

5.5 Detailed Process Mapping

Continuous Improvement activities are like a crime investigation in that both rely on the collection of evidence. Can you imagine watching a detective drama where the detectives did not visit the scene of the crime and gather evidence? As well as not being very entertaining, it would also not have a great deal of plausibility. Similarly, CI work is only ever effective if it involves the collection of evidence in the area where the problem or opportunity is based. The Japanese have a word called 'Gemba,' which translates to 'real place.' I have read that Japanese detectives go to 'Gemba,' but suffice to say you often hear within work environments, terms such as 'Gemba Walks' or 'Going to the Gemba' as if they were some sort of revelation. Let us be clear, if you a leader, CI practitioner or just want to find out what really going on and engage with people, there is no substitution for putting on your personal protective equipment (PPE) (assuming it's a manufacturing environment), going to where the action is happening and then asking about, observing and measuring things.

A desk is a dangerous place from which to view the world

John Le Carré

Detailed Process Mapping is a way of doing this in a structured way. In Chapter 3, SIPOC (Suppliers, Inputs, Process, Outputs, Customers) was described as a way of understanding the scope of the problem area and customer requirements. This is a form of Process Mapping as is Value Stream Mapping (described in Chapter 7). **Detailed** Process Mapping can be undertaken by following these steps:

  i. 'Go See' for yourself, do not take things for granted.
 ii. Get data, take measurements, use check sheets.
iii. The data we gather usually takes two forms:
   a. Hard data (often process-driven data – observations, Measurements and Quantities, Facts [Black and White]).
   b. Soft data (often people-driven data – opinions, witnesses, experiences, quotations).
   c. Both types of data will be relevant to gaining an understanding of the area and issues (Figure 5.9).

Like icebergs most of the problem is usually hidden 'below the surface.'

Factory 1 Process Map

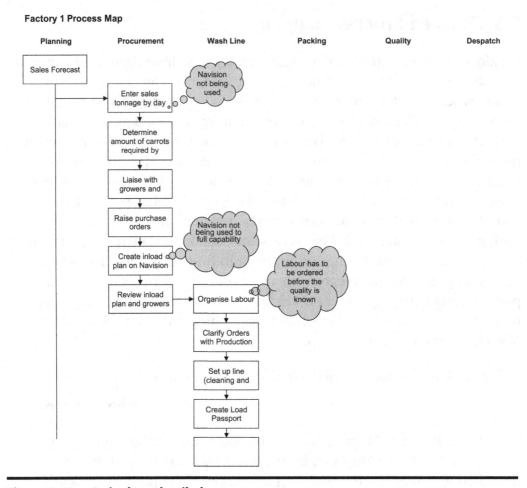

Figure 5.10a   Swim lane detailed process map.

Get to the source of the problem by asking lots of open questions to get 'below the surface.'

Ask clarifying questions to pin point the possible issues and their root causes.

iv. Draw a process flow of the process you can see and annotate it accordingly with your findings.

v. The process flow diagram can be organised into 'swim lanes' to show the interactions between teams and departments (Figure 5.10a and Figure 5.10b).

vi. Analyse the data by asking the following questions:

   a. WHAT is the issue or concern?

   b. HOW much is the impact (amount, variance from target or standard)?

   c. HOW often does it occur (hourly, daily, weekly)?

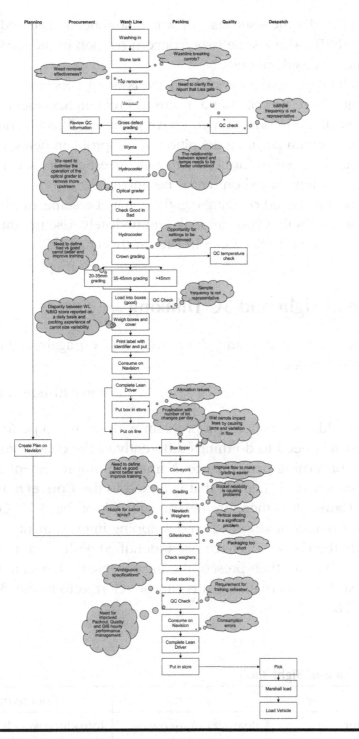

Figure 5.10b   Swim lane detailed process map.

    d. WHEN did the issue start or was first noticed (date and time)?

    e. WHERE did/does the issue/concern happen in the area/process under consideration?

    f. WHO may have an impact on the issue or concern?

vii. Use the above to write out a 'Focused Problem Statement' that incorporates all the information you have gathered. Effective problem solving relies on an accurate definition of the problem being worked upon. This can be used in further root cause investigation (see Section 5.7).

viii. Make decisions based on data – be impartial.

ix. Take actions based on data, e.g. there may be some 'quick win' improvements that you can make immediately. Use the impact effort diagram shown in Section 5.10 later in this chapter.

5.6 Line of Sight and 3C Thinking

> Insanity is doing the same thing over and over again and expecting different results.
>
> **Albert Einstein (maybe!)**

In order to address a concern (a problem with regard to performance), the process will need to do things differently to the conditions that led to the concerning performance. Namely, an improvement action (**Countermeasure**) is needed that is linked to the **Concern** as it addresses the (root) **Cause**. It is therefore helpful to think of the '3Cs' (Concern, Cause and Countermeasure) when developing improvement actions. Importantly the Cause will have been identified with 'data and facts' (see Section 5.4). We can then present the improvement plan as a 'line-of-sight table' (Table 5.4). Alternatively, this can be referred to as the '3Cs' – please see Table 5.8.

Table 5.4 Line-of-Sight Table

Concern	Cause	Countermeasure
Major failure on elevator leading to 125 minutes of downtime on Line 1	Bearing Failure owing to mechanical seal failure going unnoticed	Introduce weekly Planned Preventative Maintenance check of bearing condition

5.7 5 Whys and Fishbone Diagram

Fishbone diagrams and 5 whys can be used to help determine a root cause and not just symptoms. For example, the breakdown in the example could have been caused by an overload fuse tripping; however, this was not the root cause. This could be determined by undertaking a 5 Why's analysis. The root cause is identified by repeatedly asking why and verifying each cause in the problem's location.

1. **Why did the elevator fail?**
   Because the overload fuse blew.
2. **Why did the overload blow?**
   Because the bearing had failed.
3. **Why did the bearing fail?**
   Because dirt had entered the bearing.
4. **Why did had dirt entered the bearing?**
   Because the mechanical seal had failed.
5. **Why did the mechanical seal fail?**
   Because the bearing had not been checked recently.

If the first cause is not apparent and/or there may be multiple causes a 'Fishbone' diagram can be used (Figure 5.11). This is normally preceded by a

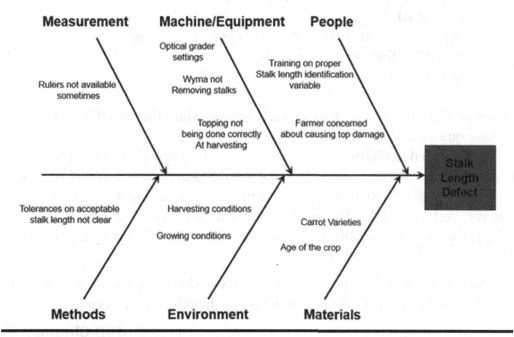

Figure 5.11   Fishbone diagram.

Detailed Process Mapping Exercise (see Section 5.5) where a Focused Problem Statement is defined put at the 'head of the fish.' Alternatively, the problem may be a 'top loss' derived from the data capture system as shown in Figure 5.6.

The team can then brainstorm possible causes and, through a process of reviewing the available data, pinpoint the most likely causes. 5 Whys can then be used to identify the root cause(s).

5.8 7+1 Wastes Review

Lean manufacturing, the CI philosophy whose greatest exponent is Toyota, can be described by the following definition:

'A Strategy, which strives to embed a culture of Continuous Improvement, whereby everyone seeks to identify and eliminate waste, enabling the business to deliver customer expectations at minimal cost and lead time.'

It is based on five defining principles:

1. Define **Value** to the Customer.
   'Voice of the Customer.'
2. Identify the steps of the **Value Stream**.
   Activities and lead times.
3. Improve the **Flow** along the Value Stream.
   Keep it moving; avoid waiting and excess inventory.
4. Move to **Pull.**
   Only make what is needed; avoid over production.
5. Strive for **Perfection.**
   Aim for zero waste.

Value is what the customer specifically wants, when they want it, at the highest quality and the least cost.

Value-added activities change the 'form, fit, or function' of the product, making it closer to the end product that the customer wants and will pay for.

Waste is any activity that is not Adding Value. It has eight categories (often called '7+1' as the 'Human Potential one was added later and, arguably, is the most important). They can be easily remembered by the acronym TIM WOOD +1 (Figure 5.12).

> When you stifle human potential, when you don't invest in new ideas, it doesn't just cut off the people who are affected. It hurts us all.
>
> **Bill Clinton**

A **7+1 Wastes** review can be undertaken by following these steps:

i. 'Gather a team of people who are familiar with area, preferably the people who work there and teach them about the 7+1 Wastes and how to see them. It will also be important to have people in the team who do not work there, as they will be able to see things with a 'fresh pair of eyes.'

ii. Visit the area and ask each person to spot wastes and list them under the TIM WOOD + 1 categories.

iii. Gather the team and ask them for their inputs and together categorise all the wastes.

iv. Using 3C thinking suggest countermeasures by using Table 5.5.

v. With the team, use the impact effort analysis (Section 5.10) to determine a prioritised action plan.

Figure 5.12   The 7+1 wastes.

Table 5.5   7+1 Wastes Table

Waste	Observations	Countermeasures
Transport		
Inventory		
Motion		
Waiting		
Overprocessing		
Overproduction		
Defects		
Wasted human potential		

5.9 Voice of the Customer

If you consider an internal or external customer to a process, there are three broad areas where you can consider the attributes of the product or outcome or service and how they relate to customer satisfaction.

Voice of the Customer Satisfaction and how it relates to Attribute Area is shown in Table 5.6.

Table 5.6   Voice of the Customer Satisfaction Levels

Attribute Area	Customer Satisfaction Level If the Attribute Is There	Customer Satisfaction Level If the Attribute Is Not There
Basic	😐	🙁
Performance	🙂	🙁
Delighters	🙂	😐

A **Basic Attribute** is something that the customer does not specify but assumes will be there, e.g. a bed with clean sheets in a hotel room.

A **Performance Attribute** is something that the customer specifies and then assesses how well the product or service performs versus their expectation level, e.g. a quiet hotel room with a balcony.

A **Delighter Attribute** is something that the customer does not specify but its provision causes a very positive reaction from the customer, e.g. a complimentary bottle of wine in the room.

A **Voice of the Customer** review can be undertaken by following these steps:

i. From a SIPOC review (see Chapter 3) identify the customers and their requirements.
ii. Categorise these into Basic, Performance and Delighter Categories.
iii. By talking to each of the customers and asking open questions gain insights into how well the process is performing (Table 5.7).
iv. Use 3C thinking to develop Countermeasures.
v. With the team, use the impact effort analysis (Section 5.10) to determine a prioritised action plan.

Table 5.7   Voice of the Customer performance Levels and Countermeasures

Attribute Area	How Well Is the Process Performing?	Countermeasures
Basic		
Performance		
Delighter		

5.10 Prioritisation Using Impact and Effort Analysis

With any improvement efforts, it is important to focus on the 'vital few' because:

■ It is effective to focus on initiatives that are going to have the highest impact with the least amount of effort.
■ Trying to do too many things can lead to failure.
■ Why expend effort and expense on matters that only give a limited return?
■ Resource is often constrained.

In the previous methods in this chapter, we have indicated that the team will have arrived at a number of possible causes or possible counter measures. At this point, the following procedure can be used to prioritise them.

1. Write the ideas on 'post-its.'
2. Decide with the team what Impact means and define what high and low means, e.g.
   - Proportion of the objective in question
   - £ Savings
   - KPI
   - Publicity
   - Credibility
   - Revenue
3. Decide with the team what Effort means and define what high and low means, e.g.
   - Proportion of the resources available
   - £ Costs
   - Manpower
   - Political capital
   - Time
   - Energy
   - Complexity
4. Draw an Impact Effort matrix on a flip chart (see Figure 5.13 above).
5. For each 'Post-it,' the team will then develop a consensus for each regarding Impact and Effort and place the post-it on the relevant quadrant of the matrix.

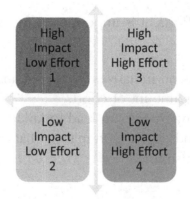

Figure 5.13   The impact effort matrix.

6. Create an action plan regarding those in Quadrant 1, followed by 2, followed by 3 that are sufficient to achieve the objective in terms of their cumulative impact or use up the available resources.

N.B. Those items in Quadrant 2 often have a low impact on the specific objective but might have a high impact on enabling factors. An example would be 'irritation' factors that have a disproportionately high impact on morale, e.g. removing unnecessary administration tasks.

5.11 Problem-Solving Levels

If the countermeasure is not known, it is likely that a further problem-solving investigation may be required to identify what is required. The degree of difficulty for each type of intervention can be represented by the following pyramid shown in Figure 5.14.

The diagram indicates the level of effort, the likely seriousness or size of the area covered by each type of problem-solving approach and the duration that the problem at each level will take to resolve.

It is not prescriptive, but in general the following guidelines are useful:

■ Choose the lowest level approach that is appropriate to the problem. You would not send someone to 'hospital' (Black belt) for a 'paper cut' (simple issue)!

Figure 5.14   Problem-solving hierarchy.

- The approaches described in the bottom two levels are used within the Operational Management System.
- The other approaches are 'higher level' and appropriate to the Strategy Deployment System.
- 3Cs and 5 Whys are considered for all action plans for any review or ritual within the Operational Management System. To illustrate, if we consider the 5 Whys example we considered earlier:
  1. **Why did the elevator fail?**
     Because the overload fuse blew?
  2. **Why did the overload blow?**
     Because the bearing had failed
  3. **Why did the bearing fail?**
     Because dirt had entered the bearing.
  4. **Why did dirt enter the bearing?**
     Because the mechanical seal had failed.
  5. **Why did the mechanical seal fail?**
     Because the bearing had not been checked recently.

And the 3Cs table is provided in Table 5.8:

We can see that Action 1 in Table 5.9 is not 'root cause' focused. By using 5 Whys and 3Cs, we can make sure it is. Team members should challenge each other to ensure this is the case. Also note that in order to arrive

Table 5.8   3Cs Table

Concern	Cause	Countermeasure
Major failure on elevator leading to 125 minutes of downtime on Line 1	Bearing Failure owing to mechanical seal failure going unnoticed	Introduce weekly Planned Preventative Maintenance check of bearing condition

Table 5.9   Action Plan

No.	Date Raised	Issue	Action (Countermeasure)	Resp.	Date Due
1	6 April	Elevator failed	Change fuse	IM	7 April
2	6 April	Major failure on elevator leading to 125 minutes of downtime on Line 1	Introduce weekly planned preventative maintenance check of bearing condition	IM	7 April

at a better action requires a more accurate problem definition under 'Issue' (Action 2).

What do we need to do to make sure the problem never happens again or
What is the 'forever fix' or
What is the 100 year fix?

■ Basic problem solving is triggered for larger operational issues or failures and/or can be used as can be used by frontline teams as the preferred tool to facilitate incremental (as opposed to step change) Continuous Improvement. This is sometimes called 'Kaizen' (Japanese word meaning 'Change for the better') or a 'baby steps' approach. The next section describes a procedure for doing this.

5.12 Basic Problem Solving

In this section, we will draw all the threads together of the previous sections into a procedure for a basic problem-solving process that covers the ringed section of the Continuous Improvement Model that was presented in Chapter 2 (Figure 5.15).

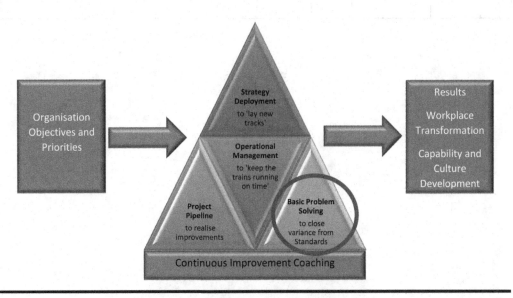

Figure 5.15   Basic problem-solving position in Continuous Improvement Model.

There are many processes for basic problem solving – this is just one example which has proven its worth with many clients. At one organisation, a Team leader (Frontline Supervisor) completed 67 in a year! The average is around 12 per year per trained employee, i.e. one per month. The process works most effectively if it is maintained as one process that everyone contributes to; it effectively helps make CI part of the 'day job' and, in time, reduces the 'noise' in the operation and achieves remarkable improvements in performance. '100 things done 1% better rather than 1 thing to achieve 100%.'

Within the procedure (Table 5.11), a tracker (Table 5.10) and a basic problem solving (BPS) document are mentioned. A template for the latter is shown in Figures 5.16a and 5.16b.

5.12.1 Basic Problem-Solving Tracker Structure

This can be maintained as an 'Excel' spreadsheet and is used so that progress can be monitored and performance analysed in routine operational review meetings such as a Weekly Operations Review.

Table 5.10   Basic Problem-Solving Tracker Structure

Ref	Date Raised	Description	Dept	Process Owner	Lead	Coach	Date Closed	Duration	Status

Table 5.11   Basic Problem-Solving Procedure

STEP	Resp.	Task Description
Trigger Condition		**Please note** that these are minimum criteria; BPS can be started for any improvement or problem. E.g. a recurring problem highlighted at the daily area meeting and agreed as an action. Minimum Criteria • > 3 hour line stoppage. • > 3 hours mechanical or electrical breakdown. • Quality Failure (e.g. 'on hold,' contamination, foreign bodies, etc.). • Major plan failures (e.g. not meeting selection time). N.B. Accidents have a separate root cause investigation procedure
1. Start BPS on Shift and Log on Tracker	BPS leader	**Please note:** BPS should be started immediately when a trigger occurs but can be started at any time, e.g. as an action at a meeting. 1. On the BPS document, complete all boxes from 'Identified by' to 'Has a similar problem been detected and resolved previously.' For now, leave the 'Team' box clear. 2. **On the BPS Tracker, complete: Ref; Date Raised; Description; Area/Line; Process Owner; Lead and Coach boxes.** 3. If you need support/advice speak to a Coach. N.B. The Governance Process starts here and the timing 'clock' starts too.
2. Review Process Flow	BPS leader	1. Go to the place where the problem occurred. 2. On the BPS document, sketch out, by hand, the process flow of machines and/or activities. 3. Gather any written evidence, check process and plant conditions. 4. Speak to people who are in the area (operators, managers, technical team, engineers, etc.) asking open questions in order to get an appreciation of what occurred and why it occurred; engage with and involve people. 5. On the BPS document, highlight where the problem occurred and also annotate the diagram with any other comments or observations. 6. As you speak to people, add them to the 'Team' box.

(Continued)

Table 5.11 (Continued)   Basic Problem-Solving Procedure

STEP	Resp.	Task Description

3. [Create Focused Problem Statement]	BPS leader	1. Stay in the area.
		2. Answering each of the questions below in turn, write out a statement on the BPS document that will enable the problem scope to be pinpointed for further investigation. **Use data and facts only.**
		  a. WHAT is the issue or concern?
		  b. HOW much is the impact (amount, variance from target or standard)?
		  c. HOW often does it occur (hourly, daily, weekly)?
		  d. WHEN did the issue start or was first noticed (date and time)?
		  e. WHERE did/does the issue/concern happen in the process under consideration?
		  f. WHO may have an impact on the issue or concern?

3. Continued	BPS Leader	N.B. The emphasis should be on obtaining the above information on the shift/day the problem occurred. Aim for 'better' as opposed to 'perfect': Attempt to get the best possible information available in the time available which will help pinpoint the root cause 'on the balance of probability.' Maintaining pace is important. If you are shift based, hand the BPS on to the next shift for continuation. **Responsibility for completion remains with the person who started it.**

4. [Are basic conditions in place?]	BPS Leader	1. Stay in the area.
		2. From the evidence you have gathered, on the BPS document, put a 'Y' or 'N' against each of the questions asked:
		  a. Has an immediate action been put in place to protect SQDCM?
		  b. Is there an agreed standard that covers the area of concern?
		  c. Is the standard clear, specific and easy to follow by the end user?
		  d. Is standard readily accessible at the Workplace?
		  e. Is the end user(s) trained (do they and the records confirm this)?
		  f. Is there evidence to show that the standard is being complied with at all times?
		  g. If applicable are machines or process plant in satisfactory condition)?
		  h. Are inputs to the area of concern within specification (material, information)?
		N.B. If you speak or correspond with anyone add them to the 'Team' box.

(Continued)

Table 5.11 (Continued) Basic Problem-Solving Procedure

STEP	Resp.	Task Description
5. Create and agree an Action Plan	BPS leader	1. Seek out and garner support from people who can carry out the actions required. 2. For all the questions above that answered 'N,' determine an action and agree it with the person who will be responsible for carrying out the action. Also, agree when it will be completed within the next 48 hours. 3. If the action is an engineering request record the reference number (if the action cannot be completed within the next 48 hours it is ok to close the action as long as there is confidence that it will be completed). 4. When the actions are complete, add 'Yes' to the relevant box. 5. Chase actions to ensure completion. **Escalate if there are problems.** 6. With regard to Questions 1–4 in this section of the BPS, a 'One Point Lesson' or 'Briefing Note' that is signed off is acceptable as long as there is confidence that the standard operating procedure (SOP) will be updated with this information at some point in the near future.
6. Has the root cause been identified and closed to the satisfaction of the process owner	BPS leader with coach	1. Meet with the process owner and, if required, a Coach, if the process owner requires advice. 2. Using the BPS Coaching tool (section 5), assess the quality of the BPS. Questions 1–3 of the coaching tool have to be a "Y" for the BPS to be closed. 3. If the criteria have not been met, add "No" to the relevant box on the BPS and add "Yes" to continue.
6. Continued	BPS Leader Coach	4. If all the criteria have been met the Process Owner should sign and date the BPS and scan it and file it in the records. 5. If all the criteria have been met the coaching tool should be completed and the score recorded on the tracker. 6. The tracker should also be updated with the Date Closed. If the root cause has been identified, then the BPS is complete and the 'clock' is stopped.

(Continued)

Table 5.11 (Continued)   Basic Problem-Solving Procedure

STEP	Resp.	Task Description

7. Root Cause Investigation 'Fish Bone'	BPS Leader	1. Turn the BPS over.
		2. With a team of people, preferably in the area where the problem occurred. Brainstorm potential causes of the Focused Problem Statement that was created in Step 3. Add them under the most appropriate category.
		3. With the team, ask them to vote on the most likely cause. Each person has three votes and can distribute them amongst their choices. E.g.
		  a. 1 on each of three choices.
		  b. 2 on 1 and 1 on another choice.
		  c. 3 on one choice.
		4. Identify the top three causes by adding up the vote and labelling **1, 2 and 3**

8. 5 Why Analysis	BPS Leader	1. For each of the top causes carry out a '5 Why' analysis by asking why progressively. Write down the question for each level and confirm that the question can be verified (i.e. the evidence gathered confirms that this is 'true'). N.B. This exercise should be carried out with team of people who have knowledge of the problem area.
9. Root cause action plan	BPS Leader	1. For each cause, write out and agree an action(s) that will rectify the root cause (who/when). 2. Chase the closure of actions and add "Yes" in the relevant box when complete. 3. Go through the points 3 to 6 in step 5.
10. Close BPS		Use the Coaching Tool to review the completion of the BPS. 1. Complete all the signatures: Leader, Process Owner and Coach. 2. Carry out points 1 to 6 on Step 6.

Basic Problem Solving Tool *(to help the resolution of problems and ensure root cause countermeasures are put in place)*

Identified by:	Date:		Dept:		Shift:		Ref:
Team:			Lead:		Coach:		

Describe the Problem:

Which KPI is affected and needs to be improved: | Has a similar problem been detected and resolved previously?

Process Flow: Go to the Workplace and sketch out the local process flow of where the problem occurs (machines and/or activities). Highlight the problem area

Focused Problem Statement: *Answering each of the questions below in turn write out a statement that enables the problem scope to be pin-pointed for further investigation

1. WHAT is the issue or concern?
2. HOW much is the impact (amount, variance from target or standard)?
3. HOW often does it occur (hourly, daily, weekly)?

4. WHEN did the issue start or was first noticed (date and time)?
5. WHERE did/does the issue/concern happen in the are/process under consideration?
6. WHO may have an impact on the issue or concern?

*Data and Facts Only

Are basic conditions in place? Check at the Workplace (A "Y" requires evidence)	Y or N?			Y or N?
1. Has an immediate action been put in place to protect SQDCM?		5. Is the end user(s) trained (do they and the records confirm this)?		
2. Is there an agreed standard that covers the area of concern?		6. Is there evidence to show that the standard is being complied with at all times?		
3. Is the standard clear, specific and easy to follow by the end user?		7. If applicable are machines or process plant in satisfactory condition?		
4. Is standard readily accessible at the Workplace?		8. Are inputs to the area of concern within specification (material, information)?		

Action Plan: If any of the answers above are No please define the action for each

Ref	Action Description	Who	When	Ccmp?

Has the root cause been identified?	Yes or No?	Closed to satisfaction of Process owner?	Yes or No?	Continue?	Yes or No?
Process owner Signature:		Date:		Please continue on reverse if not closed	

Figure 5.16a   Basic problem-solving templates and procedure on A3 paper.

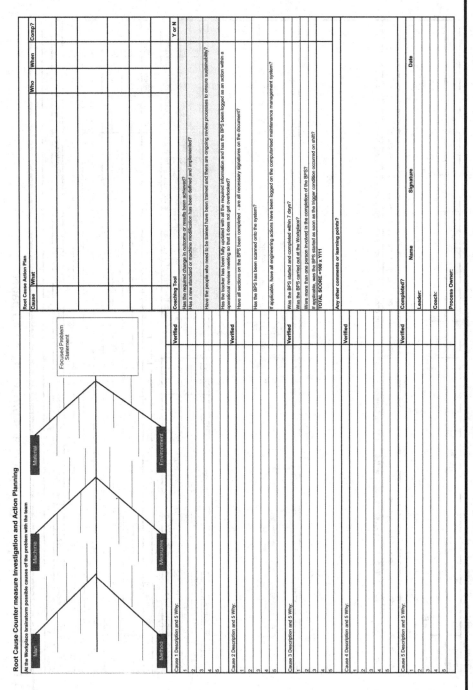

Figure 5.16b Basic problem-solving templates and procedure on A3 paper.

5.13 Standard Routines

For 'improved ways of doing something' ('Countermeasures') to be implemented effectively they need to 'stick,' i.e. become the routine way of doing something until an improvement is identified.

The following diagram illustrates the 'Standard Routines' cycle that ensures that this sustainability is achieved (Figure 5.17).

Standards are arguably the most important aspect of a Sustainable Continuous Improvement culture as they define the necessary behaviours to assure excellent results.

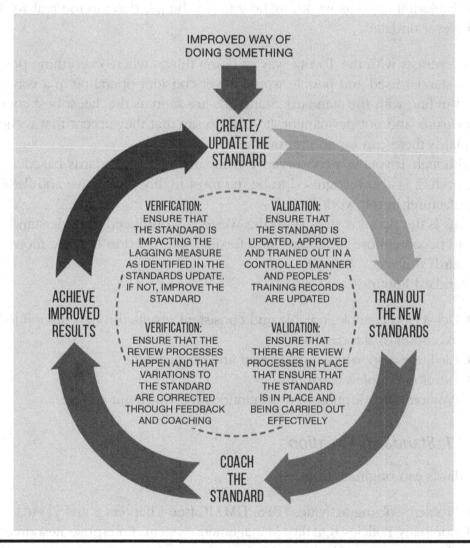

Figure 5.17   The standard routines cycle. Source: The Chemical Engineer October 2018.

A lot of people in many organisations tend to have a rather jaundiced view of Standards seeing them as one or more of the following:

■ Bureaucratic.
■ Something to 'leave on a shelf' until the auditors come around. A 'poacher gamekeeper' relationship.
■ Infringing our creativity and/or individuality.
■ Imposed from above ('not invented here').
■ Something that the Quality or Technical department does but not us (in Production).
■ 'Irrelevant to us as we know how to get the job done in the real world.'
■ Never updated.

This contrasts with the Toyota way of doing things where everything possible is standardised and people would never consider operating in a way that is not in line with the standard. Standards are seen as the 'latest best countermeasure' and not permanent. It is fair to say that they accept that without standards there can be no improvement.

Although Toyota is a conservative company with a standards-based approach, it is also recognised to be the most highly productive and flexible manufacturer in the world.

This is the paradox that we in the Western World need to understand, and to become more productive and flexible, you need to become more standards driven.

Standard Routines:

■ Deliver predictable, reliable and consistent results through disciplined execution of standard work.
■ Facilitate ownership, involvement and engagement.
■ Develop people's capability.
■ Promote the adoption of a Continuous Improvement culture.

5.13.1 Standards Creation

Standards can originate from:

■ Problem-solving activities (BPS, DMAIC [see Chapters 5 and 7] etc.).
■ Company Policies (Quality Management System, Enterprise Resource Planning system, Health and Safety, etc.).
■ Operational Management System.
■ Strategy Deployment System.

■ Continuous Improvement Tools and Methodologies (5S, FMEA, TPM [see Chapters 5 and 7], etc.).

For standards to be effective, they need to comply with three key characteristics. This is shown in the following diagram (Figure 5.18).

Relevant	Team Agreement	Easy to Understand
The Standard developed clearly links to a SQDCM priority of the organisation	The people who are going to use the Standard have been fully involved in its development and have agreed to its content	Both the training documentation and any checklists or guides should be easy to follow both from a user and observer points of view

Figure 5.18   Three key characteristics of standards creation.

Standards Creation Steps are provided in Table 5.12.

Table 5.12   Standards Creation Steps

Preparation	• **The Standard developed clearly links to a SQDCM priority of the organisation.** • Decide who is going to do what regarding the development of the standard. • Pinpoint 'what is' and 'what is not' going to be covered by the standard.
Understand the 'as is' situation	• **The people who are going to use the Standard have been fully involved in its development and have agreed to its content.** • Undertake a detailed process mapping review of area or carry out basic problem solving to identify what standards are required. • Determine the cycle times and the amount of labour/resource to carry out the current procedure. • Ensure that Safety and Quality aspects are prioritised ahead of productivity improvements.
Remove waste	• Use the 7+1 Wastes to identify and eliminate, combine, reduce or simplify wasteful activities.
Define the new standard	• **Both the training documentation and any checklists or guides should be easy to follow both from a user and observer points of view** • Identify and agree on the new standard way of working. • Write it up in consultation with relevant interested parties/experts. • Pilot the new way of working to confirm it works. • Achieve approval with relevant stakeholders.

5.13.2 Train the New Standard

1. Brief the team that there is a new or updated standard.
2. If necessary, develop presentations and training events to support the implementation.
3. Train end users and their line managers in the why, what and how to of the standard and ensure they understand.
4. Through observation, testing and coaching on the job ensure people are competent to carry out the standard at their place of work.
5. Confirm that training matrices that highlight the required number of skills and people are created and updated and visible in the area. The following template is recommended (Tables 5.13 and 5.14).

Table 5.13 Training Matrix

Name	Standard 1	Standard 2	Standard 3	Standard 4	Standard 5
John	U	U	U	L	L
Jane	L	I			
Jim	U	U	U	U	U
Julie	U	L	L	L	U

Table 5.14 Training Matrix Definitions

(None)		Cannot Perform the Task
I		Can perform with help
L		Can perform solo
U		Can train others to perform

It is recommended that this be visible on a board in the work area with photographs of the team members. This raises the profile and the levels of ownership.

5.13.3 Coach and Assess the Standard

1. Ensuring compliance with standards is a key responsibility of frontline supervisors. Build into the 'day job' and leadership standard work, e.g. 'Managing by Walking Around.'

2. Develop practice measure KPIs on the local line board and on the SQDCM board to help verify standards are being used accurately and to raise the profile of standards.
3. Raise and agree actions within the operational management system review meetings, if standards are not being followed.
4. Adopt a GROW Model coaching approach to help people become better at applying standards.
5. Recognise operators for good performance.
6. Observe and listen for opportunities to improve the standard, involve the operator.
7. Identify training and development needs.

5.13.3.1 Results Review

Within the day-to-day use of the Operational Management System, identify where standards are not meeting requirements and instigate problem-solving activities where required.

5.13.3.2 Health Check

The following checklist can be used to review the effectiveness of Standard Routines within an area and identify areas for improvement (Figure 5.19).

Standard Routines Health Check			Scoring:		
			1	Requirement met	
			0	Did not meet requirement	

Team:		Assessor:		Date:				

No.	Observation Requirements	Assessment			Comments
		Score	YES	NO	
1	The standards required within the area are linked to the SQDCM Objectives of the operation and policies of the company				
2	The people who are going to use the Standard have been fully involved in its development and have agreed to its content.				
3	The Team leader has developed a comprehensive list of standards for his/her area which cover all aspects of the Operation				
4	The standards are located in the area to allow easy access for the team and/or a reviewer				
5	A training matrix exists, showing competency levels and gaps, and is displayed in the area				
6	A training plan is followed that ensures that the skills mix across the team is sufficient to cover holidays and all forms of absence				
7	Training is carried out by the Team members and competence is assessed by other team members				
8	During daily operations Standards are displayed by the team to enable easy confirmation.				
9	Should a standard not be able to be achieved then there is a clear escalation procedure to enable the team to alert the Team Leader				
10	The Team Leader and other members of the management team visit the lines/areas regularly to assess compliance				
11	Team Leaders practice a coaching style with their teams to help them build competence on tasks and compliance				
12	The team fully own their standards and see them as the 'latest best way' and a foundation to improve				
13	The team generate improvements of standards through suggestions, BPS and other forms of problem solving (e.g. DMAIC)				
14	Compliance with standards is tracked on the SQDCM Boards				
	Total				
	% Compliance				

Figure 5.19   Standard routines health check.

5.14 5S

5.14.1 The Objective

To organise your workplace to improve safety, productivity and product quality.

5.14.1.1 How to Do It?

The 5Ss originate from five Japanese words, which describe the aspects of good housekeeping. They can be translated into English as Sort, Set, Shine, Standardise, Sustain.

5.14.1.2 Sort Out What Is and What Is Not Needed in the Workplace

Use a red tag procedure if there is a query about their priority/fate. Tag items where there is a doubt, move them to a quarantine area, review if they have been used within a month and make a decision about their fate. Figure 5.20 shows an example of a 'red tag' (Table 5.15).

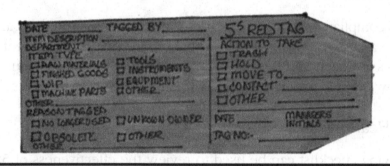

Figure 5.20   Red tag for 5S.

Table 5.15   Sort Categories

Priority	Frequency of Use	How to Store
Low	< Once per year	Throw in a skip or store in a distant place
Medium	> Once per month < Once per year	In the factory but separate from place of work
High	Daily	At the place of work

5.14.1.3 Set Items in Order

Set means that the tools, materials, change parts and consumables in the area should be located so that everything is easy to find, to keep organised and to clean. 'A Place for everything and everything in its place.' Shadow Boards are very useful for storing items locally. Figure 5.21 shows one for change parts.

5.14.1.4 Shine the Area

Shine means to thoroughly clean the area and remove and eliminate all forms of contamination. It is then to make this activity part of the routine cleaning of the area with, possibly, inspection and lubrication routines being carried out by the operators in the area – this will highlight abnormalities and promote ownership of the area by the team.

5.14.1.5 Standardise the Area

Standards will need to be created for how the area should look and how it should be maintained in that condition – see Create and Train out stages of Standard Routines earlier in the chapter.

5.14.1.6 Sustain the Gains

Standards compliance and the cleanliness and organisation of the area will need to be assessed as part of the normal Operational Management System routines – see Coach and Results stages of Standard Routines. Figure 5.22 shows how 'Sustain' acts like a 'chock' to sustain 5S improvements.

5.14.1.7 Health Check

The following checklist can be used to review the effectiveness of 5S within an area and identify areas for improvement (Figure 5.23).

Figure 5.21   Shadow board. Source: A1 Signs

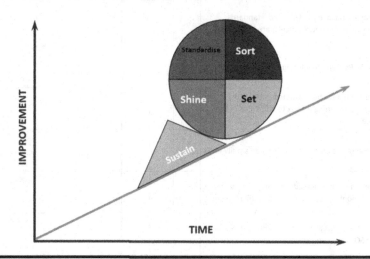

Figure 5.22   Sustain.

No.	Observation Requirements	Score	YES	NO	Comments
	5S Health Check				**Scoring:**
					1 Requirement met
Team:	Assessor:	Date:			0 Did not meet requirement
		Assessment			
1	Raw material and packaging that is not needed has been removed from the area				
2	Equipment and tools that are not needed have been removed from the area				
3	Any equipment that is not needed and still in the area has been red tagged and is due to be removed shortly				
4	The equipment and floor layout has been set out and marked logically to optimise safety and flow				
5	Tools and equiment are stored on shadow boards or indicated positions close to the workplace				
6	Raw material and packaging are stored in indicated positions with clear min and max levels				
7	The Area is clean and free from debris				
8	Visual management is neat and tidy and up to date. Cleaning records are shown on the SQDCM Board in the Area				
9	Clear Workplace photo based standards operating procedures (SOPs) are in the Area				
10	The SOPs were developed with the team				
11	The team have been trained in the SOPs - there is a training matrix to show this in the Area				
12	The area is audited vs the SOPs on a daily basis				
13	The SOPs are reviewed on a regular basis (at least monthly) to see if they are still relevant				
14	Improvements are captured and included in the SOPs				
	Total				
	% Compliance				

Figure 5.23   5S health check.

Chapter 6

Strategy Deployment

Our goals can only be reached through the vehicle of a plan.
There is no other route to success

Pablo Picasso

Figure 6.1   Strategy deployment.

6.1 Why Is Strategy Deployment Undertaken?

This manual has taken an unashamedly 'bottom-up' approach. This is borne
from experience of how Continuous Improvement (CI) develops within most
organisations that I have worked with over the years and what I believe is
most effective. In considering the six stages of the Continuous Improvement
Journey mentioned above, there is a logical case for reordering the sequence
as in Figure 6.2.

Within organisations that pursue this approach, there is often a big fan-
fare at the start which then fizzles out owing to the lack of engagement at
the shop floor level or if the leader that started it moves on for whatever reason. This is not to say that the 'bottom-up' approach does not need a plan,
it absolutely does. It's just that this can come from the Business Analysis
rather than the Strategy Deployment Process. It's also about just getting on

DOI: 10.4324/9781003244707-6

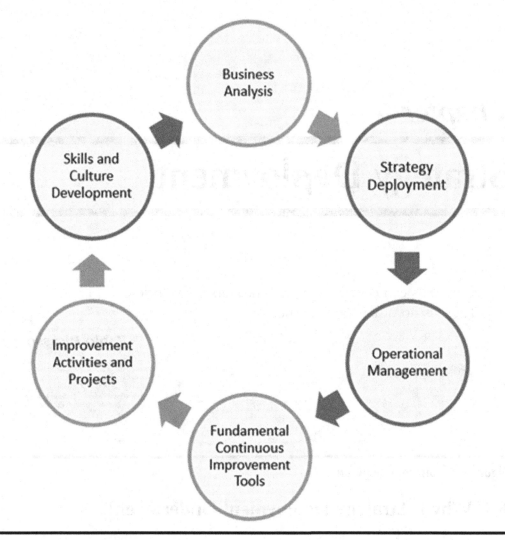

Figure 6.2 'Top-down' Continuous Improvement Journey.

with things, incremental improvement, heading in the right direction and overcoming obstacles as you come across them, navigating with a compass rather than a map!

The reason for Strategy Deployment is principally to turn CI into a 'strategic weapon' that incorporates all areas of the organisation in an aligned strategy that will keep it winning in the marketplace. It is also about making breakthrough improvements and/or changes in direction. A useful way to consider this is to imagine creating a machine that for every £1 you put into it gives you £3 back! This removal of waste and higher sales can fund further investment in innovation and growth which can fund further investment in people. This is shown in the 'Fly wheel model' in Figure 6.3.

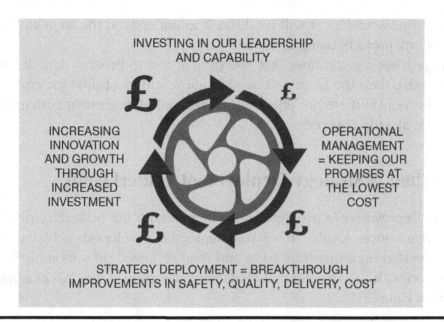

Figure 6.3   The Flywheel model. Source: The Chemical Engineer.

Ultimately, effective Strategy Deployment delivers success including a sustainable Continuous Improvement Culture.

6.2 What Is Strategy Deployment?

Strategy Deployment is a Plan, Do, Check, Act cycle for a whole organisation where the 'Plan' is the Strategy of the organisation: it is a 3–5 year plan for organisational success. The process can be represented by the six steps shown in Figure 6.4.

This process takes input from the business, the customer, the employee and the process that the senior leadership team will then use to identify potential projects for the CI pipeline.

In the early part of the process, the senior leadership team will need to consult with several of their business stakeholders. For this to be successful, it is important to allow sufficient time and engage the correct members of the organisation's team to make this happen effectively. Without input from

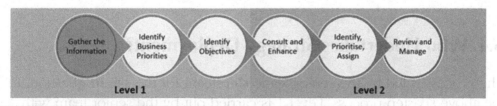

Figure 6.4   Strategy deployment process.

senior business leaders, it will be difficult to understand the strategic importance of any projects being identified.

The process also assumes that you have access to process data. If this doesn't exist, then the team will need to allow sufficient time for process data collection. If there are effective Operational Management Systems, this should be already covered.

6.3 When Is Strategy Deployment Undertaken?

Strategy Deployment is usually closely aligned with the budgetary process of an organisation. Ideally, a 3–5 year strategy is developed each year which is then revised on a quarterly basis and then reviewed on a monthly basis. Integration with the Operational Management System is key. An example is shown in Figure 6.5.

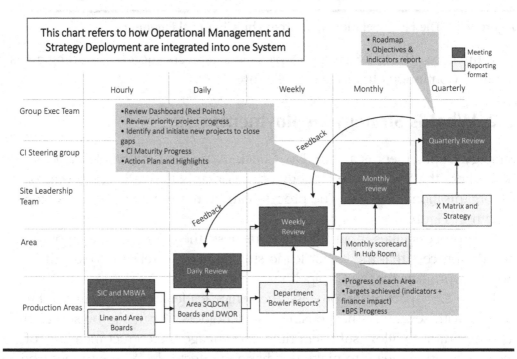

Figure 6.5   Integrated operational and strategy deployment system.

6.4 Who Undertakes Strategy Deployment?

The process is led by the senior leadership team for the site in question. In the above six-step process, Level 1 is carried out by the senior team with involvement of the whole organisation at Level 2.

It is important for each person in the organisation to know what the strategy and priorities of the organisation are and how their role links in with this. Communication and widespread involvement in the process are important features of an effective Strategy Deployment system.

6.5 How to Undertake Strategy Deployment

6.5.1 Gather the Information

Voice of the Customer – Make contact with customers and customer facing colleagues to understand market trends and evolving customer wants and needs. Carry out the analysis of market and customer data, e.g. Complaints (Figure 6.6).

Voice of the Business – Meet with senior executives and leaders to gain insights into the growth, profitability and policy aspirations of the organisation.

Voice of the Process – Carry out comprehensive analysis of KPI and loss trends to determine strategic opportunities.

Voice of the Employee – Make contact with colleagues and analyse employee survey data to understand the areas of concern and opportunity.

Figure 6.6   Gather the information.

6.5.1.1 Voice of the Customer

The wants, needs and satisfaction levels of current and future customers should have the highest priority when determining the future direction of the organisation.

A Strategy Deployment workshop with customer facing colleagues (e.g. Marketing, Sales, New Product Development, Logistics, etc.) should be prepared for and held. The preparation should include:

1. Plotting the numbers of customer complaints for the last 12 months.
2. Presenting this data as 'Complaint Reason' Pareto chart.
3. Plot the top reason as a time series plot to review trends.
4. Repeat this process for other KPIs such as 'On Time in Full' to customer performance.
5. Also meet with customers and customer facing colleagues and carry out 'Voice of the Customer' conversations (see Chapter 5, Section 5.9; Figures 6.7–6.9).

At the workshop, ask Marketing to present information on the market segments that the organisation is currently operating in and aspires to operate in. Information on competitor performance in these areas will also be of great value.

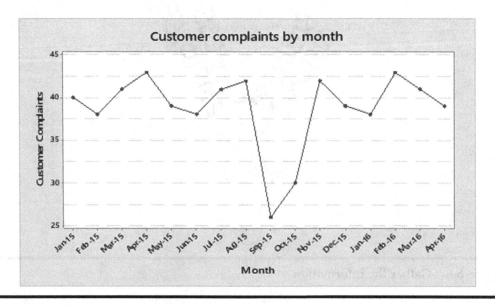

Figure 6.7   Time series plot of customer complaints.

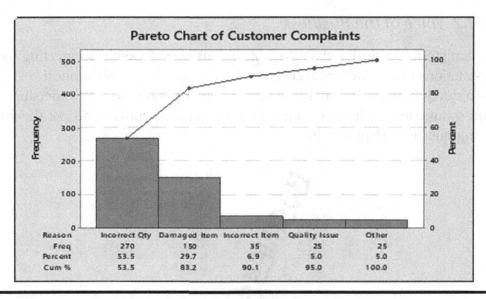

Figure 6.8   Pareto chart of customer complaints.

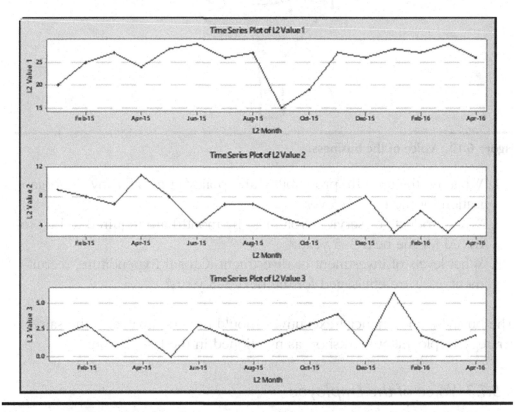

Figure 6.9   Time series plot of customer complaints top reasons. Source: Grant Beverley.

6.5.1.2 Voice of the Business

The long-term survival and success of the business depends on meeting the expectations of the owners and senior executives of the organisation.

To develop an operational strategy, the organisation's senior leadership team should approach the business and financial executives and ask the following questions (Figure 6.10).

Figure 6.10 Voice of the business.

1. What are the growth, profitability and policy targets for my site/organisation for the next 3–5 years?
2. What products or services volumes (by month) are required to be produced for the next 3–5 years?
3. What levels of investment or divestment (Capital Expenditure, recruitment, etc.) are envisaged for the next 3–5 years?

The business and financial executives should then be invited to the same Strategy Deployment workshop as mentioned in the last section.

6.5.1.3 Voice of the Employee

The people employed within the organisation will have much valuable information on where the issues and opportunities are. Their engagement and involvement in the process will help ensure the long-term success of the strategy. Prior to the Strategy Deployment workshop, a combination of formal data such as Employee Surveys and Health and Safety data should be compiled in combination with holding many informal conversations with colleagues in order to gain insights (Figure 6.11a).

Figure 6.11a Voice of the employee.

It is helpful to invite employee representatives such as trade union or work council members to the workshop.

Prior to the workshop trend, understand attendance data and accidents by creating time series plots for the last 12 months with loss reasons shown in Pareto charts (Figure 6.11b).

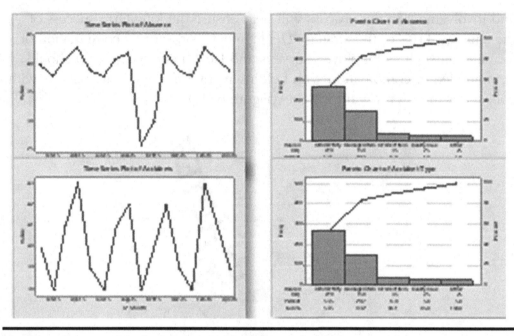

Figure 6.11b Graphical analysis of attendance and accident data. Source: Grant Beverley.

6.5.1.4 Voice of the Process

The Quality, Delivery and Cost (QCD) KPIs and loss data capture systems developed within the Operational Management System (Chapter 4) should provide information to help identify the key loss areas (Figure 6.12).

Figure 6.12   Voice of the process.

Prior to the workshop, prepare QCD KPI and Pareto charts on monthly trends and loss areas, respectively. This should be at a 'high level,' i.e. sufficient for the leaders of the organisation to understand where the key challenges are (Figure 6.13).

1. Prior to the workshop trend and understand Quality, Delivery and Cost by creating time series plots for the last 12 months with reasons shown in Pareto charts.
2. The Pareto charts should 'cut and dice' the information into reasons and also locations.
3. The reasons could be why the KPI did not achieve 100% (e.g. '% On Time in Full') or zero (e.g. Costs).

A 'Loss Tree' approach is a particularly powerful way of reviewing this area. When we evaluate Loss, we compare it with 'perfect,' i.e. Zero Losses. **'Excess' is anything additional to 'perfect' use of resources**, e.g. less than 100% OEE, 100% yield, 100% productivity, etc.

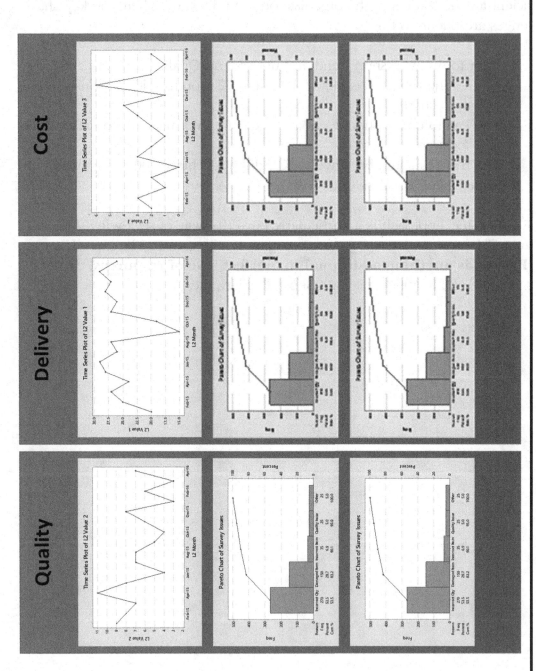

Figure 6.13   Graphical analysis of quality, delivery and cost KPIs.

Levels 1 to 4

Table 6.1   Levels 1 to 4

Level 1	Level 2	Level 3	Level 4
Excess COGS site	Excess COGS area	Production line or sub-area	Plant
			Process
			People

Level 5 'Plant'

Table 6.2   Level 5 Plant

Level 5
Mechanical breakdowns
Electrical breakdowns
Set-up/changeovers
Planned maintenance – technicians
Planned maintenance – operators
Minor stops
Waiting for materials
Planned operational stoppages
Unplanned operational stoppages
Rate loss
Not required for production
Cleaning and hygiene

Level 5 'People'

Table 6.3   Level 5 People

Level 5
Sickness
Agency labour
Overtime
Unplanned leave

Level 5 'Product'

Table 6.4   Level 5 Product

Level 5
Rework
Scrap/write off
End-to-end yield
Breakdown spares
Environment
Utilities

- For each level 5, there may be further subcategories such as Gas, Electricity and Water for Utilities.
- For each level 5, there needs to be a Unit of Measure (UoM) that can be costed directly, e.g. line hours for Changeovers or $ for Overtime.
- For each of UoM, the definition of Loss (or Excess) and how it is measured needs to be identified and agreed.
- The costing mechanism should be discussed and agreed with the Senior Financial Manager on site. There should be a linkage with the budgeting process.

Steps:

1. Set up a team: The process is typically led by a senior manager or CI practitioner with a cross functional team of representatives for each area.
2. The definitions of each of Loss Unit of Measure and the cost of each should be developed and agreed.
3. Create a spreadsheet with the following headings (Table 6.5).
4. Set up data capture systems if required.
5. Collect the data for **a full year** and populate the spreadsheet (Table 6.5).
6. Present the data using a pivot table and Pareto charts to illustrate a total excess cost for the site and how it breaks down between the areas.
7. Review with the senior management team within a 'workshop(s)' and agree on areas to be targeted.
8. Please note that the process typically takes some weeks of effort to complete the first time it is done. Later versions will be quicker if the data capture processes are in place.

Table 6.5   Loss Tree Spreadsheet Structure

Factory	Area	Line	Group	Loss	Sub Cat	UoM	Loss/UoM	Loss Qty	Total Loss
Factory 1	Spreads	1	Plant	Set up/changeovers	Blue	Hours	$1,000	200	$200,000

6.5.2 Identify Business Priorities

1. At the Strategy Deployment workshop, the team should firstly brain-storm all the ideas that come from presentation of the data collected in Stage 1. A SWOT chart can be used to prompt ideas (Figure 6.14).

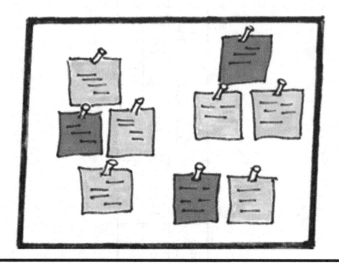

Figure 6.14   Priorities.

2. The ideas then should be grouped into areas ('affinitised') with a name.
3. The named areas then can be prioritised using an impact/effort matrix.
4. Three to six maximum business priorities can then be chosen and given an engaging description such as 'To be brilliant at the basics.' Each priority would be aligned with one of the SQDCM areas.

6.5.3 Identify Objectives

1. At the same or a follow-up workshop, the team will then identify what KPIs are needed to deliver the objective (Figure 6.15).
2. The team will then identify what targets have to be achieved by each quarter of the next year and annually for each subsequent year for the priorities to be realised.
3. It is important to limit the number of KPIs to the minimum required to meet the priority; three to four per business priority is a good rule of thumb. Each KPI should indicate a senior team member who will be accountable for delivery.

At the end of this first section of the process, the senior team would have achieved the outline of strategy that they will now engage with the rest of the organisation.

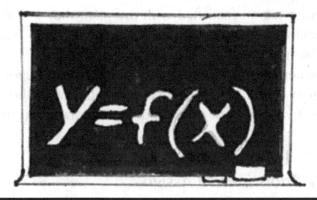

Figure 6.15   KPIs.

6.5.4 Consult and Enhance

The consultation process with the rest of the organisation is sometimes called 'catchball' as it is an iterative process involving the operational teams. The senior team will ask them how an objective can be achieved. The operational teams will come back with an outline plan which will often then prompt enhancements to the strategy. This back and forth process promotes engagement and plan effectiveness (Figure 6.16).

Figure 6.16   Consultations.

When the senior team is satisfied with the plan, they will then present it back to the executive team and aim for 'sign off.' The final outcome can then be linked with budgets and operational plans.

Although this iterative process may be slower than traditional planning processes, it is very much more effective and in line with the well-known sayings 'Measure twice and cut once' and 'Perfect planning prevents poor performance.'

6.5.5 Identify Prioritise and Assign

Once the strategy has been agreed, the operational teams are then tasked with identifying detailed plans of how the objectives will be realised (Figure 6.17).

Figure 6.17 Impact effort matrix.

This process will deliver a prioritised Continuous Improvement and strategic project plan that can be presented on a large visual management board and/or X Matrix (Figures 6.22 and 6.24). The following worked example illustrates how this is achieved.

In this example, there is a key Business Priority to 'Fulfil Growing Market Demand.' Let's assume that Overall Equipment Effectiveness (OEE) on Line 1 links in with this priority and to meet the KPI objective, the average weekly OEE (last 52 weeks) of the line has to increase from 65% to 80%. A step change! If we continue 'business as usual,' we will not achieve this objective, so a series of improvement projects are required. This approach can be applied to all SQDCM KPIs (Figure 6.18).

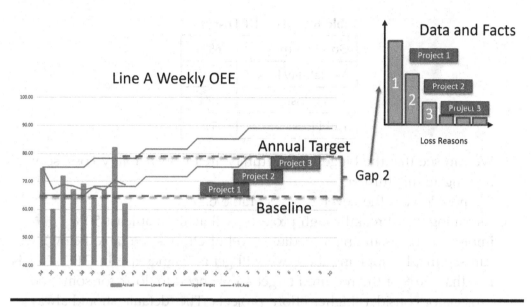

Figure 6.18 Improvement projects to achieve strategic objective.

6.5.5.1 *Identify*

1. Firstly, we look at the weekly trend (time series plot) for the last 12 months and decide what is the best baseline period. If the trend is falling or rising, it would be wise to take the last quarter average only. For a flat trend, it would be more robust to use the whole year.
2. Then we look at the Level 1 losses for the baseline period (Figure 6.19; Table 6.6).

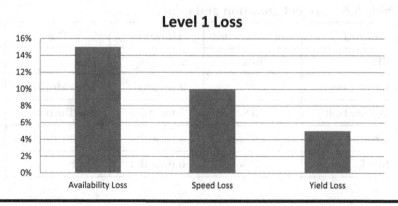

Figure 6.19 Level 1 losses.

Table 6.6   Level 1 Losses

Good Output	65%
Availability loss	15%
Speed loss	10%
Yield loss	5%

3. We can see that the biggest opportunity area is Availability Loss, so we investigate this further.
4. We now look at the Level 2 losses (Table 6.7)
5. Assuming that 'breakthrough projects' will achieve at least 50% improvement (assuming a medium level of effort – see table below), we can see that by applying these we will get a 7% increase in OEE. This is less than 50% of the required target so we need to 'look for some more' projects or consider 'higher effort' projects. The 'default' should always be to see if lower effort projects and Basic Problem Solving can deliver the objectives before considering DMAIC or A3 (Table 6.8).

Table 6.7   Level 2 Losses

Category	Loss	Opportunity
Changeovers	6%	3.0%
Breakdowns	5%	2.5%
Waiting for material	3%	1.5%
Other	1%	
Total	**15%**	**7.0%**

Table 6.8   Project Duration and Effort

Method	Improvement	Duration	Effort
BPS	10%	2 weeks	Low
Kaizen event	25%	2 weeks	Low/Medium
Yellow belt	50%	3 months	Medium
Green	60%	4 months	Medium/High
Black	66%	6 months	High

6. Looking at Level 2 for Speed Losses, we can get another 4.5% from Yellow Belt projects focused on Ambient and Frozen Products, which leaves us 4.5% to find (Table 6.9).

Table 6.9   Yellow Belt Project Contribution 1

Category	Loss	Opportunity
Frozen	7%	3.5%
Ambient	2%	1.0%
Citrus thick	0.5%	
Citrus shred	0.5%	
Total	**10.0%**	**4.5%**

7. Looking at the third loss category gives us another 2% of opportunity. Therefore, the total opportunity identified is 7 + 4.5 + 2 = 13.5%, i.e. a short fall of 1.5% on our target (Table 6.10).

Table 6.10   Yellow Belt Project Contribution 2

Category	Loss	Opportunity
Start-up loss	2%	1.0%
Reject Loss	2%	1.0%
Label errors	0.5%	
Citrus shred	0.5%	
Total	**5.0%**	**2.0%**

8. Using higher level project (green belt) for the Changeovers, Frozen and Ambient, we are able to achieve our target, i.e. 15% (Tables 6.11 and 6.12).

Table 6.11   Green Belt Project Contribution 1

Category	Loss	Opportunity
Changeovers	6%	3.6%
Breakdowns	5%	2.5%
Waiting for material	3%	1.5%
Other	1%	
Total	**15%**	**7.6%**

Table 6.12   Green Belt Project Contribution 2

Category	Loss	Opportunity
Frozen	7%	4.2%
Ambient	2%	1.2%
Citrus thick	1%	
Citrus shred	1%	
Total	**10.0%**	**5.4%**

9. This is now the suggested list of projects (Table 6.13)

Table 6.13   Project List

Project	Loss	Opportunity	Type
Changeovers	6%	3.6%	Green
Breakdowns	5%	2.5%	Yellow
Waiting for material	3%	1.5%	Yellow
Frozen	7%	4.2%	Green
Ambient	2%	1.2%	Green
Start-up loss	2%	1.0%	Yellow
Reject loss	2%	1.0%	Yellow
	Total	**15%**	

10. It would be prudent to also consider high effort projects like Black belts and even CAPEX on top of this to make sure that the target is exceeded. **The highest priority is BPS ('business as usual') activity which should be progressed to maximise all of the possible incremental gains and ensure solid foundations.**

6.5.5.2 Prioritise

11. The next task is to agree the projects' priority order with the Senior Leadership team at a review meeting (step 5 of Strategy Deployment) by agreeing a method of prioritisation through reviewing the Effort and the Impact and then plotting them on an Effort Impact Matrix. The criteria for 'effort' should be agreed and could include factor such as:

12. Effort: Cost, man-hours, complexity, 'politics,' duration, governance, availability of skilled staff (Figure 6.20).

High Impact			Changeover CAPEX? Frozen Ambient	
Medium Impact		Breakdowns Waiting for material Start up Loss Reject Loss		
Low Impact	BPS?			
	Low Effort	Medium Effort	High Effort	

Figure 6.20   Impact effort matrix.

6.5.5.3 *Assign*

13. Once the priority order of the projects has been agreed by the Senior Leadership team, the next step is to review and agree who is going to (a) sponsor the project (accountable); (b) lead the project (responsible) and (c) coach the project (train and coach).
14. If the skills are available, then above roles should be assigned.
15. If the skills are not available, then the above roles should be assigned and the relevant training or outsourcing is factored into the plans.
16. The project charter for each project then should be developed and agreed. The process is summarised in Figures 6.21a and 6.21b.

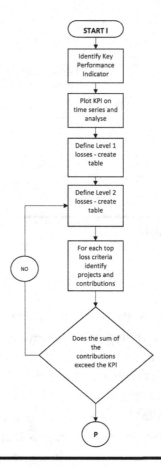

Figure 6.21a   IPA process – identify.

6.5.6 Review and Manage

The plan will only deliver if it is properly reviewed and managed.
The following elements are key:

■ A coherent communication strategy.
■ Visual Management of the whole strategy (Figure 6.22).
■ Monthly recording delivery of high-level SQDCM charts or 'bowler' charts.
■ Monthly review of progress by the organisation's leadership team (Figure 6.23).
■ Quarterly review of the plan by the organisation's team and key stakeholders.
■ Objectives and deliveries are linked into personal development reviews and annual appraisals.

An X matrix such as that shown below can be used to communicate the strategy and individual project links back to the Goals and Business Priorities (Figure 6.24).

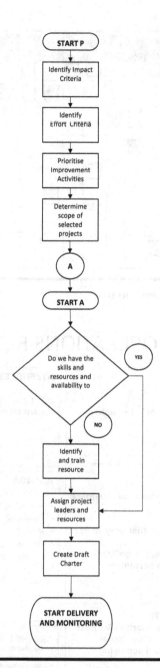

Figure 6.21b   IPA process – prioritise and assign.

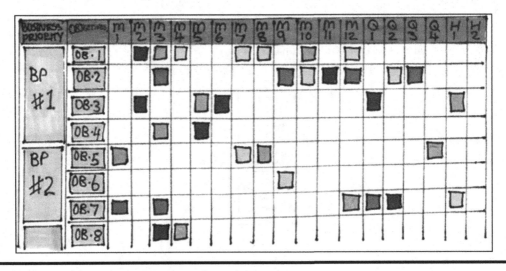

Figure 6.22   Strategy deployment board.

MONTHLY OPERATIONS REVIEW TOR

DURATION: 90 mins

FREQUENCY: Monthly (first Monday of the month)

LOCATION: Board Room

ATTENDEES:

Site Leadership Team
 Board Members

OBJECTIVES:

- To review last months performance of business areas
- To review performance trends
- To identify and action any events that may impact upon business performance.
- To ensure that the Business Strategy is on Track
- To identify further improvement opportunities.
- To agree priorities for the next week
- Every Quarter – review plan

AGENDA   **(Mins)**

- Action Log Review..10
- Review of Priority KPIs and Project Charters.......... 40
- Productivity Savings plan update...........................10
- Review of 2 LSS Projects by invitation.... 20
- Priorities and AOB... 10

INPUTS
- Monthly 'KPI chart' progress
- Updated Project Charts/QUAD reports
- Action Log

OUTPUTS
- Agree priorities for next Month (Top Three)
- Updated action log

GROUND RULES
- Meeting should be 'snappy', action orientated and last no more then 90
- Attendance is compulsory; send a deputy if you cannot attend
- Be on time, the meeting will not wait for you
- Ensure you set realistic timescales for action points and you complete them within your set timescales
- Be prepared;
    - Understand key issues & root cause before the meeting
    - problem solving before the meeting

Figure 6.23   Example of monthly operations review terms of reference.

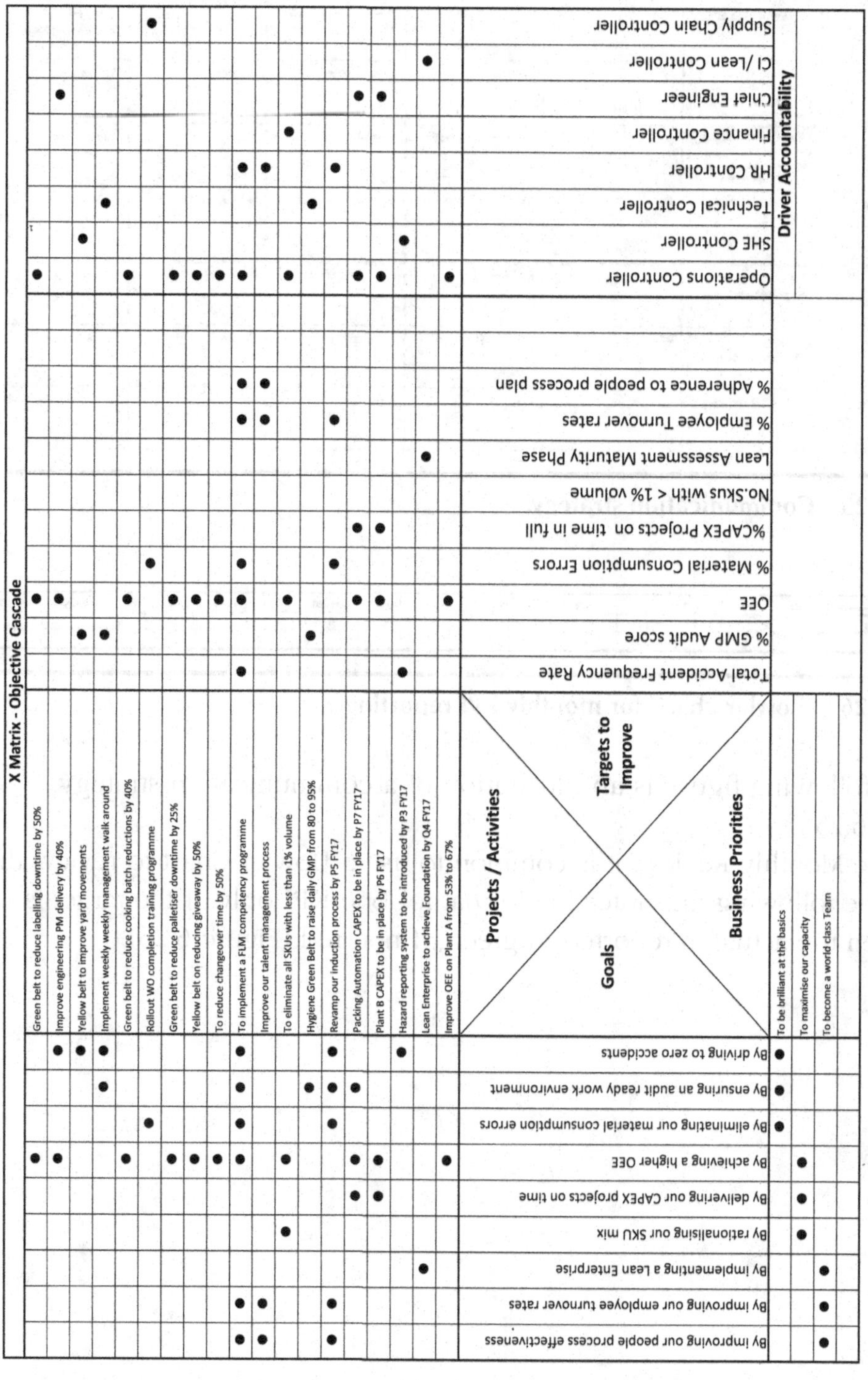

X Matrix - Objective Cascade

Driver Accountability
- Supply Chain Controller
- CI/Lean Controller
- Chief Engineer
- Finance Controller
- HR Controller
- Technical Controller
- SHE Controller
- Operations Controller

Targets to Improve
- % Adherence to people process plan
- % Employee Turnover rates
- Lean Assessment Maturity Phase
- No.Skus with < 1% volume
- %CAPEX Projects on time in full
- % Material Consumption Errors
- OEE
- % GMP Audit score
- Total Accident Frequency Rate

Projects / Activities
- Green belt to reduce labelling downtime by 50%
- Improve engineering PM delivery by 40%
- Yellow belt to improve yard movements
- Implement weekly weekly management walk around
- Green belt to reduce cooking batch reductions by 40%
- Rollout WO completion training programme
- Green belt to reduce palletiser downtime by 25%
- Yellow belt on reducing giveaway by 50%
- To reduce changeover time by 50%
- To implement a FLM competency programme
- Improve our talent management process
- To eliminate all SKUs with less than 1% volume
- Hygiene Green Belt to raise daily GMP from 80 to 95%
- Revamp our Induction process by P5 FY17
- Packing Automation CAPEX to be in place by P7 FY17
- Plant B CAPEX to be in place by P6 FY17
- Hazard reporting system to be introduced by P3 FY17
- Lean Enterprise to achieve Foundation by Q4 FY17
- Improve OEE on Plant A from 53% to 67%

Goals

Business Priorities
- To be brilliant at the basics
- To maximise our capacity
- To become a world class Team

Business Priorities (Goals)
- By driving to zero accidents
- By ensuring an audit ready work environment
- By eliminating our material consumption errors
- By achieving a higher OEE
- By delivering our CAPEX projects on time
- By rationalising our SKU mix
- By implementing a Lean Enterprise
- By improving our employee turnover rates
- By improving our people process effectiveness

Figure 6.24 X matrix.

What	How	To Whom	Who	When – Next one	Frequency	Measure of effectiveness
Strategy Briefing	Briefing events (groups of circa 50).	All on site	Exec	Start early FY17 complete by week 8	Once per year	Feedback questions on key points plus Exec walking tours
A3 Quarterly Communication	Prepare report and issue on Site and area noticeboards following quarterly Exec review	All	GM and CI Controller	Next Quarter	Quarterly	Walking tour feedback
A3 Monthly Communication	Prepare report and issue on site and area noticeboards following monthly Exec review	All	GM and CI Controller	Next Month	Monthly	Walking tour feedback
Newsletter Update	Newsletter update prepared	All	GM	From start of FY17	Bi Monthly	Walking tour feedback
Table Talkers	Update in meeting rooms and canteens	All	HR Lead	From start of FY17	Bi Monthly	Walking tour feedback
Strategy Go See Walks	Speaking to employees at place of work	All	Business Effectiveness Team	From start of FY17	Weekly	% Assessment Score
Cascade Briefings	Brief of last month's results	All staff	Exec	From start of FY17	Monthly	Feedback at meeting

Figure 6.25 Communication strategy.

By Reducing the number of accidents	FY20	FY21		Jul-20	Aug-20	Sep-20	Oct-20	Nov-20	Dec-20	Jan-21	Feb-21	Mar-21	Apr-21	May-21	Jun-21
No. of Accidents		0	Target	0	0	0	0	0	0	0	0	0	0	0	0
		3	Actual												

Figure 6.26 'Bowler chart' for monthly KPI reporting.

The following figure is an illustration of a communication strategy (Figure 6.25).

At the Monthly Review, it is common to use a Bowler Chart to review the KPIs. The following illustrates the format for one KPI only. If the target is met, then the actual is reported in green, if not, red (Figure 6.26).

Chapter 7

Improvement Activities and Projects

The biggest room in the world is the room for improvement.

Helmut Schmidt

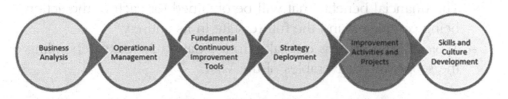

Figure 7.1   Improvement projects and activities.

In this chapter, several approaches and tools that are commonly used within improvement projects and activities are introduced. As this manual is about the fundamentals of Continuous Improvement (CI), guidance on the 'why, what, when and who aspects of the tools' is given and then as regards 'how' an outline process is described. Where appropriate, sign-posts to recommended books, etc. that will provide deeper instruction are given in Chapter 9.

7.1 Value Stream Mapping

7.1.1 Introduction

Value Stream Mapping (VSM) is a technique which can be applied to operations in manufacturing, service and public bodies to gain real-step changes in performance.

DOI: 10.4324/9781003244707-7

Essentially, it is a systematic method based on Lean Thinking that enables a representative team from the various parts of the supplier and customer organisations to identify:

- The activities (making and information) that the organisation uses to produce a range of products/services.
- How long goods or services take to be delivered to the customer to meet their requirements. This is called the Lead Time.
- What proportion of these activities is value adding and what proportion are waste? We define value-adding activities as those that the customer is, ultimately, willing to pay for.
- An action plan that identifies measures that can be put in now to reduce waste and variability and therefore save costs. Sometimes the diagnostic process can stop here.
- If required, the team can then develop a Future State Map. This allows the team to identify via a 'brown paper' map the following:
  - A prioritised list of actions that need to be undertaken to achieve the future state.
  - The financial benefits that will be obtained for each of the actions being completed and the future state in its entirety.
  - Typically, the process can take from 1 day to 2 weeks depending on the scope and deliverables of the VSM.

7.1.2 Lead Time Reduction

Cost is reduced by Lead Time Reduction. Slow processes are wasteful processes:

- Product and materials that do not flow straight through the facility must be moved, counted, stored, retrieved and moved again and may be damaged, exceed its 'shelf life' or become obsolete.
- Warehouse staff and stock control personnel are required to manage the inventory and deal with problems.

- If a quality problem arises, a large amount of product is put at risk.
- A larger factory with more equipment and people must be used for a given capacity.

Value Stream Mapping addresses all categories of waste.

How do we measure the rate of flow?

- The answer comes by comparing the amount of *value-added time* (work that the customer would recognise as necessary to create the product or service) and the *total lead time* (how long the process takes from start to end).

$$\text{Process Cycle Efficiency} = \frac{\text{Value Added Time} \times 100}{\text{Total Lead Time}}$$

In many processing companies, it is common for process efficiencies to be in the order of 1% or 2% compared to the best practice levels of 35%. There are substantial opportunities for improvement.

7.1.3 Waste Identification

Please refer to Chapter 5, Section 5.8. This described the definition of value and the '7+1' categories of waste.

7.1.4 Value Stream Mapping Team

A Value Stream Team must:

- Have a leader.
- Have cross-functional representation from all key areas of the value stream.
- Include relevant subject–matter experts and process specialists.
- Include suppliers and customers where appropriate.
- Be able to commit to spending 100% of their work time during the period of the VSM exercise as if they were on annual leave.
- Have ground rules to both contribute and be open and honest about issues and opportunities. It is more about the conversation than the map (Figure 7.2).

Figure 7.2 A team working on a VSM.

7.1.5 *Which Value Stream Should Be Worked upon?*

Typically, VSM targets an individual product (or service) or closely related group that represents the majority of the effort that operations experiences in terms of:

- Order frequencies or
- Order volumes.

It can be useful to think of categorising products or services into the following groups:

- Runners – regular ongoing predictable demand.
- Repeaters – ongoing demand with medium predictability.
- Strangers – sporadic but generally low demand; hard to predict.
- Aliens – very irregular, low demand; extremely hard to predict.

Strangers and *Aliens* can cause significant disruption and wastes if run through processes that have been designed to handle *Runners* and *Repeaters*. If this occurs, the impact of these should be considered during the VSM.

By using a Pareto chart, we can identify the Runners and Repeaters to work on, as either a single product or a group. This is called Product Quantity (PQ) Analysis.

7.1.6 Value Stream Data

These data are collected by the team on the shop floor and in the offices where the work happens:

- Demand
- Process steps
- Process times
- Output levels
- Work-in-progress (WIP) levels
- Cycle time
- Lead time
- Set-up times
- Downtime
- Speed losses
- Defect rates
- Overall equipment effectiveness (OEE)
- Manning levels
- Available time
- Capacities
- Value-added and non-value-added activities
- Planning and control systems
- Lines of Communication

7.1.7 Calculating WIP Time

$$\text{Takt Time} = \text{Available Hours per day}/\text{demand per day}$$

$$\text{WIP Time} = \text{Work in Progress} \times \text{Takt Time}$$

7.1.8 Current State Map

The team creates this on 'brown paper' on a wall in a room that has been reserved for the entire VSM activity period; typically up to 2 weeks (Figures 7.3 and 7.4).

VSM steps (please note all data should be collected from the shop floor by the team – the rule is that *it must be* observed).

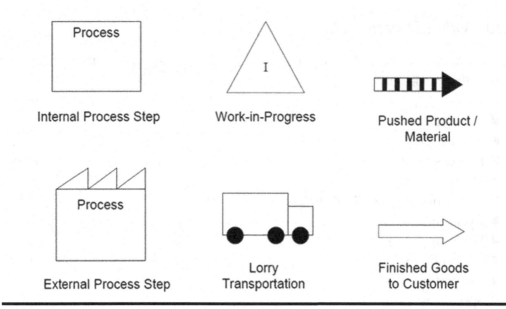

Figure 7.3   Symbols to use on map. Source: Claudius Consulting Ltd.

1. Define and agree on the project including identifying and agreeing who your customer.
2. Identify the Value Stream to be mapped using PQ analysis.
3. Write down customers, suppliers, process steps, work-in-progress (WIP) holding points and departments on post-it notes.
4. Lay out customers, suppliers, process steps and WIP holding points onto the brown paper.
5. Lay out departments onto paper.
6. Connect all steps and departments with communication lines and material/information flow lines.
7. Record levels of demand and order frequency. Aim to show general demand as a minimum.
8. Record WIP levels sitting in front of each process step (this can be an average over a suitable period of time).
9. Record output levels per day and Takt Time (this can be an average over a suitable period of time).
10. Calculate WIP Times.
11. Write down Process times for each step.
12. Calculate Overall Value-Adding Time.
13. Calculate overall Lead Time.
14. Calculate Process Cycle Efficiency.
15. Record Set-up times (CO times) for each step.

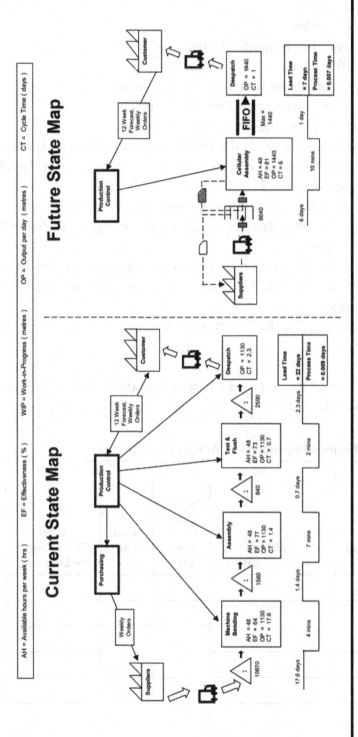

Figure 7.4   A current state and future map. Source: Claudius Consulting Ltd.

16. Record Uptime.
17. Record Speed losses.
18. Record Defect rates.
19. Record Overall Equipment Effectiveness.
20. Record Staffing levels.
21. Make note of available time and shift patterns.
22. Record capacities (current %) for each step.
23. Record current planning and control systems.
24. Summarise current state and identify problems that can be seen.
25. Identify Value-Added and Non-Value-Added activities (TIMWOOD+1 Wastes – sees Chapter 5).
26. Identify potential Continuous Improvement projects and activities and other improvement initiatives and prioritise using an Impact/Effort process (see Chapter 5).
27. Create a future state map after improvement ideas are implemented.
28. Summarise current state vs target future state and process cycle efficiency changes.
29. Create an action plan for improvements needed to achieve a future state.

This is a reminder of the Action Plan Structure described in Chapter 5, Section 2 (Table 7.1).

Table 7.1   Continuous Improvement Action Plan Structure

Area	What (KPIs)	How (Countermeasure)	Where (Plant, Dept, Line, etc.)	When (Due Date)	Who (Responsible for Delivery)	How Much (to Improve the KPI from x to y)
Safety						
Quality						
Delivery						
Cost						
Morale						

7.2 CI Project Management

Governance of change is an important aspect of Continuous Improvement. This section highlights how we can ensure that the Continuous Improvement pipeline shown in Figure 7.5 is effectively managed.

7.2.1 Project Management Steps

1. Assign sponsors.
2. Assign leaders to projects.
3. Develop charters and gain approval. If there is a financial element, ensure that the rationale behind this has been approved by a Financial Manager. An example of a template is shown in Figure 7.6. DMAIC (Define, Measure, Analyse, Improve, Control) projects, typically, have a different template – see DMAIC in Section 7.3.
4. Set up effective governance review meetings with clear terms of reference. Use this forum to identify and approve new projects and ensure project delivery effectiveness during and after the project.
5. Examples of review meetings are:
   - As an agenda item on the weekly operations review.
   - A weekly CI meeting where all CI projects progress is reviewed.
   - A monthly operations review where the progress of the strategy deployment plans is reviewed including individual CI projects.
   - Individual project 'toll gate' reviews (applies to DMAIC projects – see the DMAIC section).

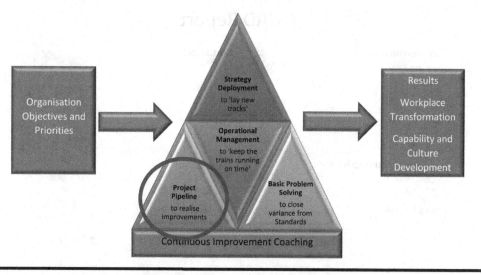

Figure 7.5   Project pipeline position in Continuous Improvement model.

Project Title: **Programme:**

Sponsor			Report Date	18th April 2022		
Project Manager			On time	●		
Process Owner			KPI Deliverable	●		
Team			Project Costs	●		
Current State and scope	Future State and rationale		Savings (£000)	FY21	FY22	Run-Rate
			Target			
			Identified			
			Actual Delivered			
			Forecast			
Progress Update since last review		Milestones			Date	Status
Key upcoming activities until next review		Key risks/ Issues, Proposed Resolution and/or Support Needed				

Figure 7.6   Project charter template.

6. Coach and sponsor projects to deliver. Ensure that the project leader is supported with both technical guidance from a more experienced CI practitioner and help removing any obstacles that arise. It is useful to issue a weekly QUAD report that can be discussed with the project sponsor. This helps maintain the pace of the project (Figure 7.7).

QUAD Report

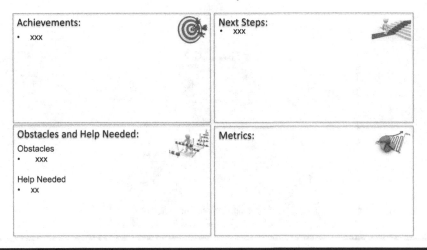

Figure 7.7   QUAD Report. *Source Grant Beverley.*

7. Focus on three outputs to achieve sustainability ('Standard Routines' – see Chapter 5, Section 5.13):
   – Result achieved.
   – An improved standard(s).
   – That has been **effectively communicated.**

7.3 DMAIC

Lean Six Sigma DMAIC is a structured problem-solving process where the project moves through each of the stages defined by DMAIC (Define, Measure, Analyse, Improve, Control). A 'toll gate' review is held at the end of each stage. DMAIC projects are delivered by certified project managers called 'belts.' To qualify for a belt, the Practitioner must attend training, pass an exam and submit a successful project to an external assessor to confirm they are able to apply their expertise effectively (Figure 7.8).

Stage	Purpose	Tools (Green and Black Belt shown in green)
Define	Identify Problem Form Team	IPA (6.5) Voice of the customer (5.9) Cost of Poor Quality Defects per Million Opportunities (DPMO) SIPOC (3) Project Charter, milestone plan and benefits (see later in this section) **Control charts using Minitab™**
Measure	Understand current process and customer requirements	Detailed Process Mapping (5.5) **VSM (7.1)** Data Capture systems (5.1) Data Reliability and Validity (**Gauge R&R) using**
Analyse	Determine root cause of the problem	Brainstorming (5.3) Data and Facts (5.4) 5 Why and Fishbone Diagram (5.7) **Scatter diagrams, regression and other graphical analysis using Minitab™** 7+1 Wastes Review (5.8) Set Up Reduction (7.6) **FMEA (7.8)**
Improve	Identify and Implement Solutions	5S (5.14) Line Balancing (7.9) Line of Sight (5.6) CI Plan (5.2) Impact Effort (5.10) TPM (7.10)
Control	Monitor and manage the process ongoing	Standard Routines (5.13) Data Capture systems (5.1)

Figure 7.8   DMAIC project stages (with chapter and section references).

For further detailed guidance, please refer to the information referenced in Bibliography.

Within DMAIC, Yellow Belt DMAIC is the 'entry level,' then 'Green Belt,' 'Black Belt' and finally 'Master Black Belt.' In many organisations with mature Continuous Improvement cultures, at least 1 in 10 employees are Yellow Belts, followed by 1 in 20 for Green Belts and 1 in 100 for Black Belts. In this way, the organisation can build up a cohort of advanced CI practitioners who can solve complex problems, deliver step change improvements and act as CI role models for the rest of the organisation. Yellow and Green Belt practitioners generally carry out projects in parallel with their usual functional roles.

DMAIC is generally used for difficult or step change problems with higher effort levels. The various levels are illustrated in Figure 7.9.

DMAIC projects are identified on the organisation's Continuous Improvement plan and are assigned to a senior manager who is called the Project Sponsor. She is accountable for delivering the project, providing resources and removing obstacles. Depending on the degree of difficulty, the project is then assigned to a Yellow, Green or Black level Project Leader who is responsible for delivering the project. If there are insufficient 'belts' available, even following prioritisation and reassignment, then a training plan will be required. It is usual for 'belts' to deliver at least two projects per year.

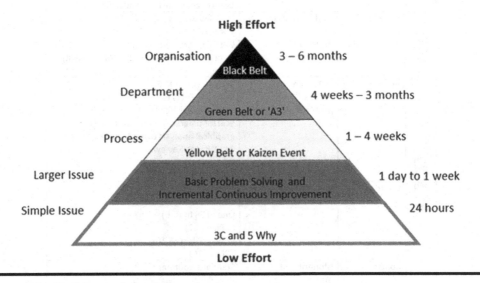

Figure 7.9   Problem-solving hierarchy.

Toll gate reviews are held between at least the Leader and the Sponsor at the end of each of the respective DMAIC stages to ensure they have been delivered satisfactorily. It is vital that the project does not move onto the next stage until all the criteria have been satisfied; strong challenge and support is required to ensure that the way forward is based on evidence and that obstacles are removed. As Yellow and Green Belts are usually done by a 'non-CI Specialist,' in parallel with their other day-to-day work, the commitment levels should not be underestimated. This is commonly a problem in organisations that do not understand the need for strong sponsorship and there is a high risk that projects will be delayed and even fail.

For trainees, a coach (Black Belt or Master Black Belt) supports the trainee during the project with specialist advice and coaching.

7.3.1 Project Governance

A Project charter mentioned below will be developed during the Define and Measure stages (Figure 7.10).

Also a milestone plan is shown in Figure 7.11. Results tracker and benefits tracker are shown in Figures 7.12 and 7.13.

7.3.2 Toll Gate Review Checklist

To successfully complete a DMAIC project, a 'story board' presentation is developed that presents the whole project and shows the critical thinking that has underpinned the project's development and delivery. Please also refer to Section 7.2 in this chapter for other CI project management guidance; regular review of progress at routine Operations Review meetings is important to keep things on track.

As indicated earlier, Toll Gates are also held at the end of each 'letter' stage of DMAIC. There follows a checklist for a Yellow Belt toll gate review:

Project Charter			
Project Title:			
Project Team		**Stakeholders**	
Role	Name	Role	Name
Project Champion			
Project Leader			
Team Members			

Problem Statement	**SMART Objective**

COPQ Summary	**VOC - Key Customers**

Scope	**Project Milestones**	Plan Date	Actual Date
	Start of project		
	End of Define		
	End of Measure		
	End of Analyse		
	End of Improve		
	End of Control/Project		

Measureable Output	**Benefits Delivered**

Figure 7.10   A project charter. Source: Claudius Consulting Ltd.

Milestone Plan: DMAIC Project xxxxx																			

Date:	22 February 2019															Resp Owner	Element Status	Comments
																	⊗ Late or Not started	
Element no	Milestone Plan Activities	22 Feb	1 Mar	8 Mar	15 Mar	22 Mar	29 Mar	5 Apr	12 Apr	19 Apr	26 Apr	3 May	10 May	17 May	24 May	31 May	7 Jun		☺ On Time
																		☺ Complete	
	Week	34	35	36	37	38	39	40	41	42	43	44	45	46	47	48	49		
Define																			
1	Project Background and Selection																	ANO	☺	Yellow belts should take < 3 months
2	Voice of the Customer																	ANO	⊗	Green Belts should take < 4 months
3	Problem Statement																	ANO	☺	Black Belts should take < 6 months
4	Objective																	ANO	⊗	Timings shown are for Green Belt and are
5	Cost of Poor Quality																	ANO	⊗	illustrative only
6	Baseline Performance																	ANO	⊗	
7	Target Performance																	ANO	⊗	
8	Stakeholder Investigation and communication plan																	ANO	⊗	
9	SIPOC																	ANO	⊗	
10	Creation of project definition document																	ANO	⊗	
11	Start weekly reporting to sponsor and coach																	ANO	⊗	
12	Toll Gate Review																	ANO	⊗	
Measure																			
13	Detailed Process Map																	ANO	⊗	
14	Value Stream Map (current)																	ANO	⊗	Green and Black Belt only
15	Data reliability and validity																	ANO	⊗	
16	Sampling technique justification																	ANO	⊗	
17	Toll Gate Review																	ANO	⊗	
Analyse																			
18	Analysis Approach																	ANO	⊗	
19	Data segmentation																	ANO	⊗	
20	Pareto Analysis																	ANO	⊗	
21	Scatter Diagrams/Regression																	ANO	⊗	Green and Black Belt only
22	Other graphical analysis																	ANO	⊗	
23	Cause and effect Analysis																	ANO	⊗	
24	5 Why Analysis																	ANO	⊗	
25	FMEA																	ANO	⊗	Green and Black Belt only
26	Toll Gate Review																	ANO	⊗	
Improve																			
27	Lean Principles Application																	ANO	⊗	
28	Improvement selection																	ANO	⊗	
29	Improvement Action Planning																	ANO	⊗	
30	Value Stream Map (Future)																	ANO	⊗	Green and Black Belt only
31	Change Considerations																	ANO	⊗	
32	Statistical Tests																	ANO	⊗	Green and Black Belt Only
33	Project Cost Saving																	ANO	⊗	
34	Toll Gate Review																	ANO	⊗	
Control																			
35	Standard operating procedures																	ANO	⊗	
36	Control charts																	ANO	⊗	Green and Black Belt Only
37	Audit plan																	ANO	⊗	
38	5S application for Control																	ANO	⊗	
39	Project handover/closure																	ANO	⊗	
40	Toll Gate Review																	ANO	⊗	

Figure 7.11　Milestone plan.

Figure 7.12   Results tracker.

Benefits Tracker   Don't type in yellow boxes

No	Item and rationale	Opportunity per annum	Week	Total	1	2	3	4	5	6	7	8	9	10	11	12
Grand Total			Planned	£0	£0	£0	£0	£0	£0	£0	£0	£0	£0	£0	£0	£0
			Actual	£0	£0	£0	£0	£0	£0	£0	£0	£0	£0	£0	£0	£0
1			Planned	£0												
			Actual	£0												
2			Planned	£0												
			Actual	£0												
3			Planned	£0												
			Actual	£0												
4			Planned	£0												
			Actual	£0												
5			Planned	£0												
			Actual	£0												
6			Planned	£0												
			Actual	£0												
7			Planned	£0												
			Actual	£0												

Figure 7.13   Benefits tracker.

7.3.3 Toll Gate Stages

Checklists of Design Phase, Measure Phase, Analysis Phase, Improve Phase and Control Phase are provided in Tables 7.2–7.6.

7.3.4 A 'Sledgehammer to Crack a Nut?'

Many Toyota Production System (TPS) devotees are not fans of the DMAIC approach; they see it as both onerous (as compared to the 'baby steps' approach of Kaizen), in some cases, elitist, i.e. top down and carried out by specialists rather than the team and, worst of all, as an opposing philosophy which in their eyes does not work. There are endless debates on professional social media between so-called experts about the merits of DMAIC versus TPS and which is the only true path.

Whilst undoubtedly, there are some DMAIC experts that act in an elitist manner (as some individuals are wont to do in all walks of life), I would respectfully counter that DMAIC is a highly effective tool (definitely not a philosophy) that if performed by or with frontline teams can produce extraordinary step changes in results that are sustained. It is the 'how' as opposed to the 'what' that is important.

On a broader, more philosophical note, I think that CI should be about what works and, as such, we should always be open to new ideas and mixing and matching our plans depending on circumstances.

Table 7.2 Define Phase Checklist

Define		Yes?
1	Has the context of the project been fully explained?	
2	Have you explained why your project was chosen in preference to others?	
3	Have you explained what prioritisation method was used?	
4	Has a sponsor, who will be accountable, for the project been identified?	
5	Is this project indicated on the Continuous Improvement plan for the factory that is regularly reviewed by the business unit team and senior leadership team (SLT)?	
6	Has a problem statement been created? E.g. 'what is wrong with what?' E.g. The delivery performance of the company is only 70% of target	
7	Has the problem statement been written from the customer perspective (internal or external)?	
8	Has a Voice of the Customer Critical to Quality (CTQ) review been completed?	
9	Are the objectives of the project SMART? E.g. The objective of this project is to reduce rework in department Z by 50% over the next 6 months	
10	Has the project objective been written out that includes a cash business benefit and Critical to Quality Targets from the Voice of the Customer?	
11	Has the project performance baseline been reviewed?	
12	Has the primary KPI (not £) of the project been identified that is aligned with your problem statement and objective?	
13	Has the Defects per Million Opportunities (DPMO) of the project been calculated for before the improvement begins?	
14	If relevant, have secondary KPIs been considered, e.g. to ensure that quality and customer satisfaction are not adversely affected?	
15	Has a Cost of Poor Quality (COPQ) been reviewed that takes account of both 'soft' and 'hard issues?'	
16	Has the COPQ £ figure been calculated and the calculation breakdown shown?	

(Continued)

Table 7.2 (Continued)   Define Phase Checklist

Define		Yes?
17	Has a Target Defects per Million Opportunities (DPMO) been identified?	
18	Is there an explanation of how the target DPMO has been determined that aligns with the project objective and potential savings?	
19	Has a SIPOC (Suppliers, Inputs, Process, Outputs, Customers) diagram review been completed that shows the SIPOC, project scope and demonstrates team involvement and critical thinking?	
20	Has a stakeholder analysis and stakeholder map review been completed?	
21	Have all the stakeholders been identified and shown on a stakeholder map?	
22	Has a RACI (Responsibility, Accountable, Consulted, Informed) diagram been created that indicates the RACI for each stakeholder and respective DMAIC stage of the project plan?	
23	Has a communication plan been developed?	
24	Has an Excel Project Definition Document been established? (Charter, Milestone Plan, Tracker, Benefits Phasing)?	
25	Has a milestone plan been created that indicates at least the milestone dates of each of the DMAIC stages?	
26	Is the outline benefits and phasing/rationale shown and the benefits phasing spreadsheet agreed with the sponsor and financial manager (FM)?	
27	Has a QUAD report been created that is being updated weekly and sent to the coach and sponsor?	
28	Are you confident that your project has the necessary support (including a support team) and resource to succeed?	
29	Are you meeting regularly with a coach for advice?	
30	Has the sponsor and coach approved the Define stage?	

Table 7.3 Measure Phase Checklist

Measure		Yes?
1	Has a Detailed Process Map been created that identifies both Value-Adding and Non-Value-Adding steps?	
2	Has a Data – valid and reliable audit been completed?	
3	Is there a statement on the validity and reliability of the data/data collection process and what you have done to ensure the data is fit for purpose?	
4	Is there a clear explanation for why the data is good enough?	
5	Is there an explanation of what you discovered during the data audit process?	
6	Is there an explanation of what precautions have been taken to improve the data quality?	
7	If relevant, are there any longer term measurement system improvements that need to be made?	
8	Has a Data Collection and Sampling plan been created?	
9	Is the communication plan developed in Define being followed?	
10	Has the milestone been updated and if there are any issues these have been actioned?	
11	Has the KPI tracker been updated and if there are any issues these have been actioned?	
12	Has the Benefits tracker been updated and if there are any issues these have been actioned?	
13	Has a QUAD report been created that is being updated weekly and sent to the coach and sponsor?	
14	Are you confident that your project has the necessary support (including a support team) and resource to succeed?	
15	Are you meeting regularly with a coach for advice?	
17	Are there explanations for what has been learnt in the Define and Measure phases of the project and what issues and evidence have been collected?	
18	Has the sponsor and coach approved the Measure stage?	

Table 7.4 Analysis Phase Checklist

Analyse		Yes?
1	Have you described how you will carry out the investigation (data analysis techniques used, who was involved, why you used this approach)?	
2	Has a Pareto analysis/Problem Segmentation been undertaken?	
3	Using the loss data generated from your data capture, have you shown the main losses/problems in a Pareto format?	
4	Have you shown that your project is focusing on the major losses/problems?	
5	Has a cause and effect review been completed?	
6	Have you demonstrated that the cause and effect diagram was developed with a team rather than just in isolation?	
7	Has a cause and effect 'fishbone' diagram which shows all the potential causes been identified under relevant categories?	
8	Is there a clear identification of the priority causes with an explanation of how these were identified?	
9	Has a 5 Why's analysis been undertaken?	
10	For the priority causes has a 5 why's exercise been carried out to a point where an action can be taken?	
11	Has each 'why' stage been verified?	
12	If the 5 whys is 'read backwards' with 'therefore' between each 'why' answer does it make sense?	
13	Is the communication plan developed in Define being followed?	
14	Has the milestone been updated and if there are any issues these have been actioned?	
15	Has the KPI tracker been updated and if there are any issues these have been actioned?	
16	Has the Benefits tracker been updated and if there are any issues these have been actioned?	
17	Has a QUAD report been created that is being updated weekly and sent to the coach and sponsor?	
18	Are you confident that your project has the necessary support (including a support team) and resource to succeed?	
19	Are you meeting regularly with a coach for advice?	
20	Has the sponsor and coach approved the Analyse stage?	

Table 7.5   Improve Phase Checklist

Improve		Yes?
1	Has an Improvement Actions list been created?	
2	Is there a description of how countermeasures have been developed (e.g. brainstorming, pilot trials)?	
3	Is there an explanation for how you have quantified the opportunity of each root cause?	
4	Is there an explanation for the decision criteria used to select improvements, e.g. show a simple impact/effort graph	
5	The improvement action plan shows by action, opportunities, benefits, completed actions (what, when, who) and future actions (what, when, who)	
6	Has an Application of Lean Principles been considered?	
7	Is there an explanation of how Lean Principles have applied such as waste identification, 5S, set-up reduction, mistake proofing, cellular processing?	
8	Have Change Management Considerations been considered?	
9	Is there an explanation for what cultural issues you have considered and addressed in your improvement efforts?	
10	Is there a 'Force Field Diagram that shows 'against' and 'for' forces that were encountered	
12	Has a line of sight table (e.g. 3Cs) been created that summarises the findings from the Analyse and Improve Phases?	
13	Has the Project cost saving and other realised benefits been realised?	
14	Does the KPI tracker show that the improvement has been sustained for at least 3 months or 30 data points (variable) of 90 data points (attribute)?	
15	Is the updated KPI tracker and £ benefits tracker shown and are both on or above target to the satisfaction of the Financial Manager?	
16	Are the soft benefits that have been obtained described?	
17	Is the communication plan developed in Define being followed?	
18	Has the milestone been updated and if there are any issues these have been actioned?	

(Continued)

Table 7.5 (Continued)   Improve Phase Checklist

Improve		Yes?
19	Has a QUAD report been created that is being updated weekly and sent to the coach and sponsor?	
20	Are you confident that your project has the necessary support (including a support team) and resource to succeed?	
21	Are you meeting regularly with a coach for advice?	
22	Has the sponsor and coach approved the Improve Stage?	

Table 7.6   Control Phase Checklist

Control		Yes?
1	Is there an explanation for what control actions have been taken?	
2	For new SOPs – is there an explanation for what new/revised work instructions have been created to ensure improvement is sustained?	
3	For new SOPs – is there an explanation for how it was developed and error proofed?	
4	For new SOPs – is there a photo of both the SOP and the training records?	
5	Is there an explanation of where and when the performance of the primary KPI is reviewed during normal operations and how this will be sustained?	
6	If 5S has been implemented are there 'before' and 'after' photos shown?	
7	If 5S has been implemented is there evidence that this is being sustained?	
8	Is there an explanation of how the project and trackers have been handed over to the process owner so that 'business as usual' can resume?	
9	Is the Process Owner satisfied with the outcome and the project has closed?	
10	Is there a Control/Monitoring plan?	
11	Is there an Audit Plan to ensure sustained improvement?	
12	Is there an explanation how you will use an audit plan or checklist to ensure your improvements are sustained in the future?	

(Continued)

Table 7.6 (Continued) Control Phase Checklist

Control		Yes?
13	Does the audit plan show who will be responsible?	
14	If things slip back is there a reaction plan and what is it?	
15	Is there an explanation for how further improvements will be identified and progressed?	
16	Is there a Project wrap up statement?	
17	Are further details given on where the project has been archived?	
18	Is there an acknowledgement/recognition given to people who have contributed to the results?	
19	Is there a description for how anything that could not be covered in the project will be picked up in the future?	
20	If there are any other recommendations are these clearly set out?	
21	Has the whole story board been presented to the senior leadership team?	
22	Has the sponsor and coach approved the Analyse Stage?	
23	If relevant, has the completed story board been sent to the examiner?	

Source: Claudius Consulting.

7.4 Kaizen Event

A Kaizen event is a rapid resolution of a problem or opportunity area that has been identified from one of the following sources and included in the organisation's Continuous Improvement plan. These are typically the areas that are 'top losses' and 'stick out like a sore thumb!'

■ Business analysis.
■ IPA review.
■ Value stream mapping.
■ Escalated basic problem solving.
■ Escalated issue from operational review meetings or team members.
■ Team 'Brainstorming' following 7+1 waste review.
■ Failure mode effects analysis.
■ Creative ideas.

The event is where a team of individuals are taken away from their regular jobs and requested to work full time (as if they were on annual leave) on a problem from 3 to 10 days. Usually these will be operators/end users from the area where the problem is occurring, support team representatives (e.g. engineering, technical) and CI Practitioners to facilitate the process if required. The onus is on making the changes and installing them during the Kaizen event with things that have to be followed up afterwards as an 'exception to the rule.' The basic problem-solving format, DMAIC or A3 Thinking format can be followed.

A typical timetable is provided in Table 7.7.

Table 7.7 Kaizen Event

Day	Morning	Afternoon
Monday	• Introduction to the problem. • Review of the objective. • Guidance on the Kaizen process. • Review of process data available and team. • Guidance on 7+1 Wastes.	• Detailed Process Mapping in the Area. • 7+1 Waste Review in the Area. • Review of basic conditions. • Sharing of observations. • Agreement of a Focused Problem Statement.
Tuesday	• Detailed Cycle Time information capture. • Other Detailed Studies.	• Detailed Cycle Time information capture. • Other Detailed Studies.
Wednesday	• Use of fishbone and 5 whys to determine root cause. • Brainstorm of possible solutions and the use of impact effort to prioritise.	• Build prototype modifications and new layouts. • Pilot in area with local team. • Adjust solutions based on findings.
Thursday	• Build prototype modifications and new layouts. • Pilot in area with local team. • Adjust solutions based on findings.	• Implement solutions in area with team. • Create Standard Operating Procedures and add to training matrices. • Identify remaining actions. • Generate detailed action plan.
Friday	• Team review findings and create a presentation setting out what they have done and what still needs to be done. • A Monitoring and Audit plan is created.	• Present back to the local senior managers in the area. • Recommend what support is needed for the gain to be sustained.

7.5 A3 Thinking

A3 Thinking is a structured problem-solving technique that is principally used by organisations that follow the Toyota Production System philosophy. It is called A3 because all the sections of the problem and the solutions are summarised on an 11″ × 17″ piece of paper. It can be performed by a leader with a team either as a project over several weeks/months or as a Kaizen event. Typically, problems are broken down into smaller elements and it is common for a number of 'A3s' to be undertaken in quick succession to achieve a greater goal.

The eight steps, with recommended tools, are shown below with references to the relevant chapter and section of this manual (Table 7.8).

In a similar way, to that as described for DMAIC, this approach emphasises that the project should not progress onto the next stage unless the

Table 7.8 A3 Methods

Stage	Tools
Clarify the problem	Data Capture Systems (Section 5.1); Detailed Process Mapping (Section 5.5) Voice of the Customer (Section 5.9) Basic Problem Solving (Section 5.12)
Breakdown the problem	Data and Facts (Section 5.4); Brainstorming (Section 5.3) 7+1 Wastes (Section 5.8)
Target setting	Voice of the Customer (Section 5.9) Identify Objectives (Section 6.3) Identify Prioritise Assign (Section 6.5)
Root cause analysis	Data and Facts (Section 5.4) 5 Whys and Fishbone Diagram (Section 5.7)
Develop countermeasures	Brainstorming (Section 5.3) Line of sight and 3Cs (Section 5.6) 5Ss (Section 5.14) Mistake proofing (see Figure 7.23)
See countermeasures through	Standard Routines (Section 5.13)
Monitor results and processes	Data Capture Systems (Section 5.1) Operational Management System (Chapter 4)
Standardise successful processes	Standard Routines (Section 5.13)

current stage has been completed to the satisfaction of the Sponsor and other key stakeholders such as the internal customer for the project. This is central to the 'scientific thinking methodology' of the approach that is underpinned by evidence and results. Rigorous analysis and challenge are required to ensure that the right problem is defined and worked upon and that the countermeasures address the root cause and achieve the targeted condition.

Crucial to A3 Thinking is that all the activities regarding the project occur, as much as possible in the location where the problem or opportunity is situated.

There are many different templates for A3; most are shown in a landscape format (Figure 7.14).

Project:	Leader:	Sponsor:	Date Started:
Site:	Area:	Team:	Date Completed:
Clarify the Problem		Develop Countermeasures	
Breakdown the Problem		Monitor Results and Processes	
Target Setting		See Countermeasures Through	
Root Cause Analysis		Standardise Successful Processes	

Figure 7.14 A3 problem-solving template.

7.6 Set-Up Time Reduction

Set-up reduction is a technique (often referred to as SMED – Single Minute Exchange of Dies) to reduce Setting up, Changeover or Resetting times to a minimum. Within many production operations, set ups are one of the greatest areas of lost time so there is a reluctance to changeover which means that 'Over Production,' one of the 7+1 Lean wastes, occurs. To reduce waste and customer lead times, it is necessary to build products in much shorter runs and level production (see Section 7.7). Rapid set-up allows the operation to increase capacity, therefore enabling the reduction of 'Over Production' waste and unit costs.

To understand the approach, there are two important categories of set-up time to understand:

■ Internal set-up activity relates to any operation which must be performed while the machine or process is shut down, i.e. not running.
■ External set-up activity relates to any operation which can take place whilst the machine or process is running.

This approach is best carried out as a Kaizen event (see Section 7.4 earlier). The steps to follow are:

1. Determine current set-up time through observation.
2. Categorise current set-up into internal and external activities.
3. Convert internal into external activity.
4. Reduce internal activity.
5. Reduce external activity.
6. Continue to reduce all elements on 'non-value-adding' basis.
7. Activity to reduce set-up further.

It can be considered in four phases (Figure 7.15).

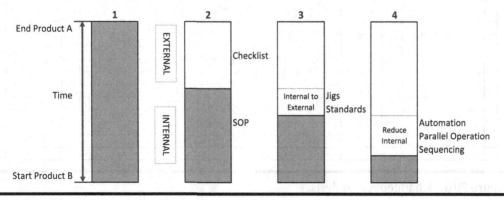

Figure 7.15   The four phases of set-up reduction.

7.6.1 Phase 1

1. The set-up reduction team reviews the production and decides on manageable sections to work on and observe.
2. The set-up reduction team identifies and lists all tasks involved in the chosen changeover type.
3. The team carries out a detailed process mapping exercise (Chapter 5, Section 5.5) to confirm the steps involved and ensure that any additional activities are identified.
4. Produce a total timeline for the chosen changeover type. This should be from the maximum running rate of product A to the maximum running rate of product B.
5. Observe a changeover, normal operating team with set-up reduction team observing and recording all the start and end times of each activity and the number of people involved for each activity. It is useful to use a video camera to record this activity.
6. Using the changeover analysis, develop a timeline for the changeover (Figure 7.16).

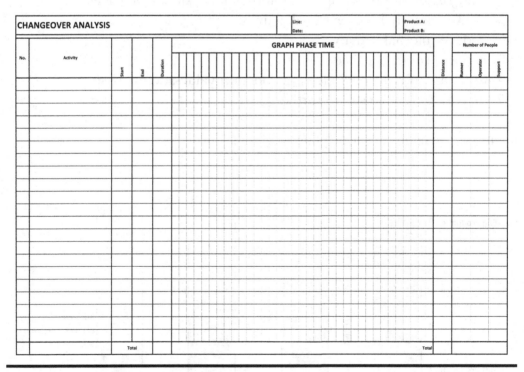

Figure 7.16   Changeover analysis.

7.6.2 *Phase 2*

1. From the analysis, the set-up reduction team categorises the activities into **Internal** and **External**.
2. The team will then identify an ideal sequence and timeline for the internal elements.
3. The team then develops a draft external checklist and internal standard operating procedure (SOP).
4. Using 5Ss develop a standard for the area that includes a 'SET' stage, e.g. shadow boards, storage of supplies and locations for materials (see Chapter 5, Section 5.14).
5. The set-up reduction team trains the local team in the changeover and confirms that they can carry it out in practice. Any adjustments and learning points are built back into the Checklist and the SOP.

7.6.3 *Phase 3*

1. From the baseline established, the objective is now to convert internal tasks into external tasks.
2. If adjustments are made on the line, these can be reduced using jigs and quick release parts.
3. Standardisation of components, ingredients and packaging formats can help reduce times as they are eliminated from the set-up.
4. Revamp the SOP and Checklists and train out.

7.6.4 *Phase 4*

1. From the baseline established, the objective is now to eliminate or reduce internal tasks.
2. If an identical machine or main element can be set up in parallel, then this should be considered.
3. Eliminate the need for manual adjustment through automation.
4. Review and improve the sequencing of the task.
5. Revamp the SOP and Checklists and train out.

7.7 Levelling the Schedule

It is common for manufacturers of processed products, such as food and drink, to prefer long runs on production lines to build batches of product. Typically, the longer the shelf life of the product stock keeping unit (SKU), the longer the production runs. This approach is based on the need to keep unit costs as low as possible as measured by traditional accounting systems, e.g. reducing changeovers reduces the amount of time the line is idle, thereby increasing labour recovery plus long production runs enables raw materials to be bought in bulk therefore reducing cost per unit.

However, this approach has the following disadvantages:

■ As product is made in batches, there is not a continuous flow of product to the customer.
■ Differences in resourcing requirements between different products can mean there are peaks and troughs of effort leading to excessive and sub-optimal use of people and other resources. These, in turn, cause Safety, Quality, Delivery, Cost and Morale problems.
■ There is increased stock in the organisation leading to cash being tied up, the need for larger premises, storage costs and the risk of spoilage and obsoletion losses.
■ The production lines do not pull at the rate of customer demand. There is a tendency to oversize equipment and lines to build batches quickly. These are more expensive to purchase, maintain and operate and are less flexible than assets that are right sized for the level of demand.

How do we address these disadvantages by improving the flow to the customer and manufacture product at a rate that matches the customer demand on a day-to-day basis?

Toyota uses an approach called Heijunka. Essentially, they level the production schedule to reduce the peaks and troughs. This levelling approach is also applicable to the process industry.

Levelling aims to create a production sequence that is aligned with customer demand as much as possible: It uses the Takt time of the product to determine the sequence and rate of manufacture.

Takt time for each product SKU item= Production hours available per day/ customer demand per day.

The available time for a 24/7 factory would be 24 hours less the 'not required for production' time.

Let's consider an example:

For a can filler running at 400 units per minute and 70% OEE it could produce:

400 × 60 minutes × 24 hours × 70% = 403,200 items or 0.2142 seconds per can.

If 200,000 were required a day for sales, the Takt time would be 24 (hours) × 60 (minutes) × 60 (seconds)/200,000 = 0.432

Therefore, it would be prudent to run the line for 0.2142/0.432 × 24 = 11.9 hours per day rather than 24 hours a day. Levelling avoids stock building and other peaks and troughs.

Table 7.9 illustrates a comparison between the two approaches.

The following is a four-step example of implementing level scheduling for a two-product company (Table 7.10).

For this two-product company, this would be the ***Fixed Repeatable Schedule*** made every day that would be adjusted to accommodate changes

Table 7.9 Long Production Runs versus Level Scheduling Comparison

Long Production Runs	*Level Scheduling*
• Aims to maximise production output so more tonnes are produced and **variances are minimised**, i.e. the more standard costs per tonnes are 'recovered.' • The day-to-day approach is 'Materials Resource Planning' (MRP) which is built up from a system of standard costing and build rates. • Works to a 'push' system of scheduling that works from forecasted customer demand, safety stocks and Economic Order Quantities (EOQ). • The production schedule and sequence changes often owing to demand and capacity changes. • Changeovers are seen as 'bad' and to be avoided if possible. Long runs are seen as 'good.'	• Aims to match daily customer demand with production capacity so that Lean Wastes (TIMWOOD +1) are minimised. • Product demand by SKU by day, by week is analysed. Products are categorised into Runners, Repeaters and Strangers. • Works to a 'pull' system where products are 'built' to a Fixed Repeatable Schedule which ideally is the same everyday but, if not, to the shortest possible repeating period that enables demand to be satisfied. • Capacity Planning uses MRP and is 'decoupled' from day-to-day operations. • The ongoing objective is to increase the number of changeovers that will still enable the production demand to be achieved. • There is an ongoing programme to reduce changeover times and associated waste. • CI aims to improve production reliability.

Table 7.10 Long-Level Scheduling Steps

Step	Example
Determine total weekly demand for each product.	• Product A – 10,000 Items • Product B – 2,500 Items Assuming batches of 500 items, this would in a 'Long Run' set-up with a weekly cycle, result in a sequence as follows (even greater if a month's product was produced each time): AAAAAAAAAAAAAAAAAAAABBBBB
Calculate the daily requirement for each product.	• Product A – 10,000/5 = 2000 Items (assumes 5 workdays) • Product B – 2,500/5 = 500 Items • Total daily production = 2,500 Items
Calculate the batch ratio and production frequency for each type of product.	• Product A Batch Ratio – 2,000/500 = 4 • Product B Batch Ratio – 500/500 = 1 • Total Production Frequency = 5
Establish a Levelled Schedule.	• BAAAABAAAABAAAAB (one batch of Product B produced for every four batches of product A).

in the volume. If the proportions of the two products changed significantly, it would be necessary to change the pattern to level the production.

The success of a level scheduling will depend on how well production changeover times are reduced (see Section 7.6 of this chapter).

Changeover performance should be a priority key performance indicator (KPI) that is reviewed and managed as part of the day-to-day operational management system.

Start-up and shutdown times and wastes should also be managed and improved upon.

Predictability, reliability and consistency of line performance are the hallmarks of a levelled production environment and underpin and, in turn, feed off of continuous improvements. A stable process is so much easier to improve than a varying one.

7.8 Failure Mode and Effects Analysis

This technique can be used in the design of a new (physical or transactional) process or to an existing one to identify and implement countermeasures that eliminate or reduce the chances of failures causing adverse impacts to the customer (Safety, Quality, Delivery, Cost and Morale).

7.8.1 Steps

1. Identify the process stages/unit operations ideally with a cross-functional team that includes frontline team members and the customer.
2. Identify the potential modes (types) of failure that impact the KPIs that have been identified to monitor the process, most commonly this is focused on quality but can be used for other KPIs.
3. Identify the potential consequence (effects) to the 'customer' of each KPI failure mode and their **Severity** (with the team determined criteria for scoring from 1 extremely low to 10 extremely high).
4. Identify the potential causes of each failure mode and their likelihood of **Occurrence** (with the team determined criteria for scoring from 1 extremely low to 10 extremely high).
5. Identify the controls that are in place to prevent or detect each failure cause and stop it going onto the next stage in the process and the likelihood of **Detection** (with the team determined criteria for scoring from 1 extremely high to 10 extremely low).
6. For each failure, calculate a Risk Priority Number (RPN) by multiplying Severity, Occurrence and Detection.
7. Identify the actions that are recommended to reduce the likelihood of the cause and/or the detection of the failure.
8. Implement the actions and recalculate the RPN.
9. If the RPN is <36, then usually no urgent action is required.

7.8.2 Example

This example is from a carrot packing factory intaking harvested carrots and then processing and packing them into bags ready for despatch to retailer customers (Figures 7.17 and 7.18).

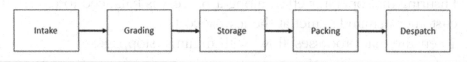

Figure 7.17 Carrot packing process.

Process Product FMEA Form														
Process or Product Name	XYZ						Prepared by: IM							
Responsible: IM							FMEA Date: 12 April			Page 1 of 1				

Process Step/ Input	Potential Failure Mode	Potential Failure Effects	SEVERITY	Potential Causes	OCCURRENCE	Current Controls	DETECTION	RPN	Actions Recommended	Resp	Actions Taken	SEVERITY	OCCURRENCE	DETECTION	RPN
What is the process step and input under investigation	In What ways does the Key Input go wrong?	What is the impact on the Key Output Variables?		What causes the Key Input to go wrong?		What are the existing controls and procedure that prevent the cause of the Mode of Failure?			What are the actions for reducing occurrence of the cause or improving detection?		What are the completed actions taken with the recalculated RPN?				
Intake	Incorrect quality received	Quality is not suitable for packing could lead to shorting of customer	8	Poor harvesting/ growing	4	Informal field samples sent through	6	192	Start Grower to Factory project	IM 1st August	Project Approved				
	Quality of carrots received is different to expected	Not having the correct resources on shift to correctly grade carrots. Line has to be slowed to accommodate which risks shorting customer	6	No field information available	4	Intake QC check once per load	5	120	Start Grower to Factory project	IM 1st August	Project Approved				
Grading	Defective carrots are not removed to correct degree	Target (<25% defects) is not achieved. Customer rejects product and issues QAS1	8	Poor training and unclear procedures	8	End of wash line test once per hour	6	384	Install more representative quality check, undertake Gauge R&R assessment of quality assessors, develop procedure and implement training programme of graders	IM (Done)	Valid and reliable test installed (once every 30 minutes). Other indicated actions also completed	8	2	2	32
Storage	Excessive storage time	Shelf life of carrots is exceeded and customer may be shorted	8	Poor stock control	2	Daily stock takes and temperature checks	2	32	None						
Packing	Incorrect labelling	Customer receives incorrectly labelled packaging and rejects product (QAS1)	8	Incorrect setting on labeller	4	Checks on start up of each product and once per hour	1	32	None						
Despatch	Incorrect picking	Customer does not receive correct order quantity and sends in QAS2	7	Picking errors	4	Orders are checked on loading lorry	1	28	None						
	Excessive storage time	Shelf life of carrots is exceeded and customer may be shorted	8	Poor stock control	2	Daily stock takes and temperature checks	1	16	None						

Figure 7.18   Carrot packing process FMEA.

7.9 Line Balancing

The purpose of line balancing is one or a combination of the following objectives:

1. Increasing Overall Equipment Effectiveness and process capacity.
2. Optimising the flow through a process bottleneck.
3. Ensuring that operator effort along a process is balanced to ensure that customer demand is met at the lowest cost.
4. To ensure that processes 'flow' with minimal stoppages.

5. To ensure that processes 'pull' in line with the Takt time of the products/services being produced.
6. Determine OEE standards and costings by product type (run rates, manning, etc.).

Line balancing in processing industries can be categorised into two main areas for manufacturing processes:

■ Automated processes where the machines dictate the throughput and the operators are essentially 'minding' the operations.
■ Labour-intensive processes where the operators are driving the throughput of the process.

7.9.1 Automated Processes

Considering a continuous packing line, the filler is (or should be) the 'bottleneck' machine, it is typically where Overall Equipment Effectiveness of the line is measured.

Overall Equipment Effectiveness = Availability × Rate × Right First Time
Availability = Uptime/Available Time × 100
Rate = Rate of line when running (units per minute)/max rate of line × 100
Right First Time = No. Good Units produced/Total Units produced × 100
Machines upstream should run faster to feed the filler all the time.
Machines downstream should run faster to take away from the filler all the time.

The aim should be to operate the filler at the maximum speed that will produce product that fulfils all the quality requirements. Ideally, the filler size will have been determined from that sufficient to accommodate the maximum daily demand in line with a levelled schedule (see Section 7.8).

For the whole line to run at optimum speed, the machines in the line should be set to run as a 'V profile' (or more like a $\sqrt{}$). This chart shows an ideal set-up with the filler at 400 units per minute (UPM) and each downstream machine at 8% more than the one in front of it and the one upstream machine at 8% more. This speed increment should be no less than 5% for optimum running (Figure 7.19).

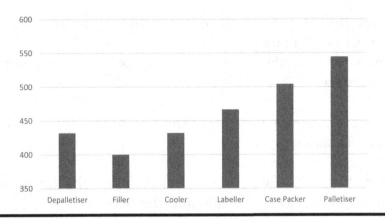

Figure 7.19 '**V profile.**'

Steps:

1. Obtain the rated speeds for each item of equipment within the process to be analysed. Do this for each product type/group.
2. Produce a flow chart of the process and include the rated speeds.
3. Produce a V curve chart as illustrated earlier.
4. Perform a series of speed studies per item of equipment and product type/group where the actual running rate is determined. This could be done for each shift too if this is believed to be a significant factor.
5. The actual speeds are then plotted on the same V curve and the gaps or losses from the design speeds can be highlighted.
6. If the V profile is deficient, maybe even at design speeds (i.e. less than 5%), then this will be highlighted by the study.
7. Investigate and identify the root causes for any deficiencies/gaps.
8. An improvement plan should then be developed and implemented to address the losses in a priority order. Capital expenditure may be required.

Product accumulation such as 'accumaveyors' may be required between stages to accommodate minor stops and changeovers. Accumulation to accommodate process failures should be avoided as this creates unnecessary inventory, takes up floor space, increases the costs and masks quality failures.

7.9.2 Labour-Intensive Processes

If we consider a quite simple process for preparing sandwiches (Figure 7.20).

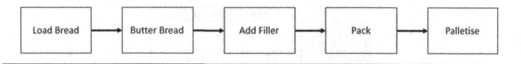

Figure 7.20   Sandwich assembly process.

To balance the line:

1. Determine the maximum number of people that can be accommodated per stage of the process.
2. Determine the maximum rate of any automatic or semi-automatic stages (e.g. packing machine). This should be the bottleneck.
3. From observation, calculate the cycle time per person per stage of the process.
4. Generate a table with unit operations and cycle times for one person.
5. From the table calculate how many people per unit operation are required to balance the line and achieve the required throughput, i.e. the recalculated cycle time must be less than the bottleneck cycle time.
6. Look for opportunities for combining activities so that all people are fully occupied during each cycle, i.e. as near as possible but not exceeding the bottleneck cycle time.

Example

1. People per stage:
   a. Load Bread: 4 people.
   b. Butter Bread: 4 people.
   c. Add Filler: 3.
   d. Pack: 60 packs per minute with one machine minder.
   e. Palletise: 4 people.
2. Packing machine can produce 60 packs per minute maximum.
3. Cycle time per sandwich per person:
   a. Load Bread: 0.9 seconds.
   b. Butter Bread: 4 seconds.
   c. Add Filler: 2.9 seconds.
   d. Pack: 1 seconds.
   e. Palletise: 2 seconds.
4. Cycle time table and cycle time chart are shown in Figure 7.21a and 7.21b.

	Cycle Time	Bottleneck Time
Load Bread	0.9	1.00
Butter Bread	4	1.00
Add Filler	2.9	1.00
Pack	1	1.00
Palletise	2	1.00

Figure 7.21a   Cycle time table.

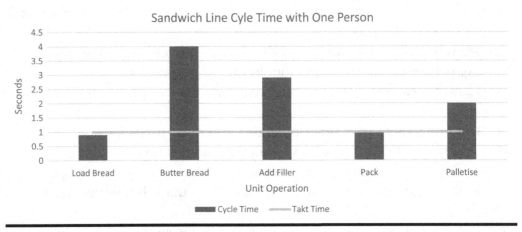

Figure 7.21b   Cycle time chart.

	Cycle Time	Bottleneck Time	People required		New Cycle Time
Load Bread	0.90	1.00	0.90	1	0.90
Butter Bread	4.00	1.00	4.00	4	1.00
Add Filler	2.90	1.00	2.90	3	0.97
Pack	1	1.00	1.00	1	1.00
Palletise	2.00	1.00	2.00	2	1.00
				11	

Figure 7.21c   Cycle time table with required number of people.

5. Cycle time table and cycle time chart with a required number of people are shown in Figures 7.21c and 7.21d.
6. Looking at this example, there is no opportunity to combine roles. The loader could also be used for replenishing the other activities with raw material.

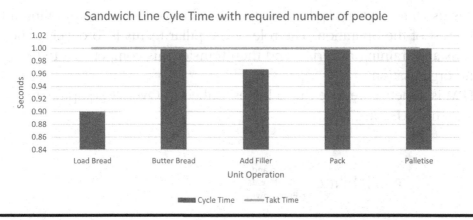

Figure 7.21d   Cycle time chart with required number of people.

7.10 Total Productive Maintenance

Total Productive Maintenance (TPM) is a holistic approach to the care of machines to ensure they perform at their optimum levels for as long as possible with the best safety quality delivery cost morale (SQDCM) outcomes. It involves the whole of the Operations team, i.e. not just the Engineering Maintenance team. There are eight areas (often called 'pillars') that it typically covers as shown in Figure 7.22.

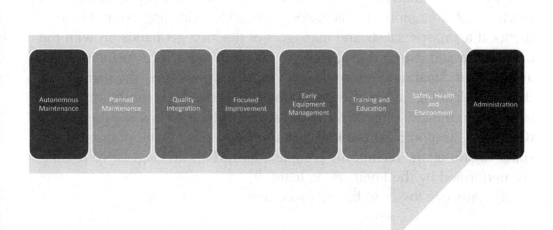

Figure 7.22   The eight pillars of TPM.

It is usual to start in a pilot area (one production line) before rolling it out to the rest of the operation. The role of the pillar teams is to develop the systems and training materials and then transfer this competence to the rest of the organisation.

TPM is aimed to reduce the '6 losses' linked to Overall Equipment Effectiveness (Figure 7.23).

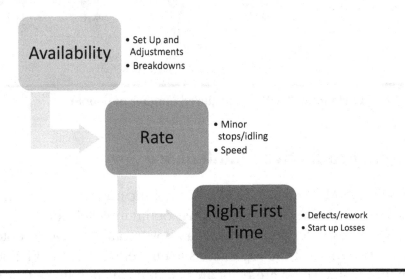

Figure 7.23   The six losses.

7.10.1 Autonomous Maintenance

This pillar focuses on Asset (machine) Care. In its simplest form, this is handing over as much of Asset Care as possible to the people who run the machines. Autonomous maintenance starts with a cleaning event where the local team, specialists and managers of the area get hands on with the target plant and strip it down, clean it, note and tag defects including leaks and wear and tear, and return the line to basic conditions. The team then develops cleaning, inspection and lubrication procedures for the operators to maintain the equipment within the scope of their technical expertise. 5S (Chapter 5, Section 5.14) is a key tool applied to ensure an optimum work space organisation. Technically complex, hazardous and legislative routines are performed by the Engineering team.

The principle losses to be improved are:

■ Set-up and Adjustments.
■ Minor Stops and Idling.

The benefits are:

- Increased ownership of the equipment by the operational team.
- Reduction of waiting for the Maintenance team as many simple adjustment tasks are carried out 'in house.'
- Increased machine life as 'forced deterioration' is reduced through early detection of problems and improved lubrication.

7.10.2 Planned Maintenance

This pillar develops the following areas:

1. Implement work order scheduling.
2. Define logical parts.
3. Build equipment list.
4. Write preventative maintenance orders.
5. Build manuals.
6. Inventory management.

The principles losses to be improved are:

- Breakdowns.
- Speed of the line.

The benefits are:

- Breakdowns reduce.
- Production is not interrupted by maintenance activities.
- Capital expenditure is reduced as the machinery life is increased.
- Spare parts holding are optimised for availability and costs of holding are reduced.

This is a specialist engineering area – please refer to the bibliography for further information. However, with regard to defining a more effective planned preventative maintenance approach, the following simple criticality analysis is recommended.

This spreadsheet approach facilitates the actions required to bring key machinery performance up to an acceptable standard.

1. For each key machine in the area, review the following using a score of 1 to 5. Multiply these scores together to give a ranking score for each machine.

IOQ (Impact on Quality): If the machine fails, how much is the quality of the product affected? E.g. fill weights, spoilage.

IOR (Impact on Rate): If the machine slows, how much is the throughput affected? E.g. How much is the rate of the line reduced; can a 'stop-gap' method be used to keep the line running?

IOA (Impact on Availability): If the machine stops, how much is line availability affected? E.g. How much downtime is caused by a failure; can a 'stop-gap' method be used to keep the line running?

FR (Failure rate): Frequency of failure. E.g. ranking in 'top loss' stoppage occasions.

RT&C (Repair time and cost): E.g. How much production is lost when it breaks down; how long does it take to repair; how much is the repair cost?

7.10.3 Example of Criticality Analysis

2. For each machine, review if the maintenance strategy for that machine is optimal (Table 7.11).
3. Make your conclusions and recommendations under the headings of People, Plant, Systems and Procedures.

Table 7.11 Criticality Analysis

Item	IOQ	IOR	IOA	FR	RT&C	Score	Priority
Depalletize	2	3	5	1	3	90	6
Filler	5	5	5	3	4	1500	1
Lidder	4	5	5	3	4	1200	2
Cooler	4	3	5	1	4	240	5
Labeller	3	4	5	4	4	960	3
Tray Pack	3	4	5	4	4	960	3
Palletiser	2	4	5	4	3	480	4

7.10.3.1 Quality Integration

This TPM pillar works to ensure that the production process involving machines and operators can detect and prevent errors as early as possible in the process.

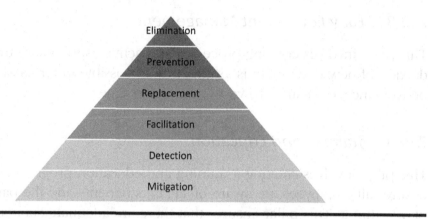

Figure 7.24 The mistake-proofing hierarchy.

The pillar team uses basic problem-solving techniques (Chapter 5, Section 5.12) to identify and implement a solution that addresses the root cause of quality errors.

Mistake proofing (Poka-yoke in Japanese) is used to design the processes and machines to eliminate errors according to the following hierarchy (Figure 7.24).

They also focus on developing systems where quality errors are automatically detected and dealt with by each unit operation. This is called autonomation (or Jidoka in Japanese).

The principle losses to be improved are:

■ Defects and rework.
■ Start-up losses.

The benefits are:

■ The cost of poor quality is reduced.
■ Quality issues are addressed with root cause focused solutions.

7.10.3.2 Focused Improvement Pillar

This pillar is responsible for developing and delivering the Continuous Improvement plan for the line based on the loss data generated. Please refer to Chapters 5 and 7 for further guidance.

7.10.3.3 Early Equipment Management

This pillar involves creating processes and activities to ensure that introduction of new equipment is as effective as possible in terms of functional performance, costs and delivery/commission times.

7.10.3.4 Training and Education

This pillar involves creating a training and education programme that ensures all employees are aware of TPM, its benefits and the part they play within it. This pillar ensures that there are adequate Standard Routines Processes (Chapter 5, Section 5.13) across each of the Pillars and Organisation as a whole.

7.10.3.5 Safety Health and Environment

This pillar involves ensuring the systems and training are in place to assure safe operation and minimal environmental impact.

7.10.3.6 Administration

This pillar facilitates the development of the support functions within the business, so they are aligned with the TPM way of working and apply the principles and techniques of Continuous Improvement within their teams too.

Chapter 8

Skills and Culture Development

We should work on our process, not the outcome of our processes. It is not necessary to change. Survival is not mandatory. It is not enough to do your best; you must know what to do, and then do your best.

W. Edwards Deming

Figure 8.1   Skills and culture development.

If you are a senior manager or executive, it is worth reading this chapter first as it provides advice and pointers for creating and sustaining the right environment for a Continuous Improvement (CI) Culture. It endeavours to link all the pieces together and signpost relevant chapters where further information is presented on the area that is of special interest to you (Figure 8.1).

The following areas are covered:

1. Managing behaviour
2. How to check if the organisation is ready
3. What if Continuous Improvement has failed a few times?

DOI: 10.4324/9781003244707-8

4. How do I keep going in the right direction?
5. How do I hook in all departments?
6. Creating the right environment.
7. Barriers.
8. The application of psychology.
9. Use of consultants.
10. How to sell Lean to the food industry.

The following passage was written by Nick Meakin who used to be my boss and is someone that I have learned a terrific amount from. I think it very succinctly describes how a leader should behave within an organisation that follows a Continuous Improvement philosophy.

> You as a 'new' manager did not need to know how everything worked and where the problems were as you had many people working in the operation who, between them, knew exactly how it worked and where all the problems were because they lived with them every day.

> One of the issues with 'traditional' control structures is that they assume first level people are lazy and are not interested. They tend to be designed to control the 3% of people who don't care about doing a good job. Reorganising to permit the 97% who do care and facilitating the removal of things that slow them down or get in the way of them doing the right thing is the fastest way to get 'better' happening. And for that, you do not need to know what is going on, you just need to be a good judge of people, a good listener, a fast learner and be able to allow things to change, i.e. you are a 'manager.'

8.1 Managing Behaviour

The following model is based on the one developed by Terry Wilson and described in his book *A Manual for Change* (Gower 1994). It illustrates that when considering what affects behaviours at all levels of an organisation that three principles are key (Figure 8.2).

■ The behaviours and performance of an organisation are directly proportional to each other and are driven by the same factors. In simple terms, an organisation with 50% 'World-class performance' will have

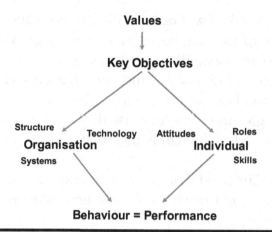

Figure 8.2   Managing behaviour.

significantly different behaviours than one with 75%. This may be obvious, but I have met many managers over the years that think that they can achieve step change in performance without changing their own behaviours.

■ That behaviours are the result of the interplay of the real values of the organisation, its objectives (strategy and policy) and organisational and individual factors. It suggests that concentration on one factor will not lead to the desired change in behaviour unless all of the factors are considered and implemented within a change programme.

■ Organisations that want to achieve sustainable higher performance must build capability in all areas as part of a coherent strategy.

If we consider some typical behaviours of shop floor workers in a poor performing company:

■ Not able to operate machinery properly because of poor training and shift cover (skills).

■ Do not take responsibility for the reliability of their machinery because they are not given accountability for it (roles).

■ Do not raise problems with management because they think that they do not care and do not know their impact on the company (attitudes).

■ Continually intervening to rectify minor stops of the equipment (technology).

■ Not having enough time to do the job properly because the team are 'thin on the ground' because of high absence caused by a poor labour planning and control and absence management (systems).

- The team do not take ownership of their performance because their team is not set up for team-based process management with highly visible results and accountability (structure).
- There is no sense of urgency as the performance and policy objectives are not understood or owned by them (objectives).
- People do not give their best because they are treated as 'human doings' as opposed to 'human beings' (values).

Hopefully, this has illustrated that 'poor' behaviours do not happen because of one isolated cause and that the successful improvement of them requires a broad-based plan of action.

8.1.1 Tips for Success

Rather than describe a one-size-fits-all approach, I have set out a list of observed good practices that I have come across in manufacturing and other organisations I have worked in as an employee or as a Continuous Improvement coach/consultant. I will deliberately work from the 'bottom to the top' of the above model.

8.1.2 Skills

Education is the most powerful weapon which you can use to change the world.

Nelson Mandela

1. Budget for and ensure that there are enough adequately skilled operatives, technicians and managers on a shift-by-shift basis to cover an accurately generated demand pattern of production, cleaning and asset care allowing for absence, holidays, training and Continuous Improvement. It is surprising how often under staffing causes problems – you would never staff a football (soccer) team with just 11 players!
2. Train and task frontline managers with the skills development of their teams, provide them with time to do this and measure their effectiveness.
3. Generate a 'Standard Routines' way of working (Chapter 5) that involves the teams in the development of their own standard operating procedures for all operational and compliance areas.

4. Train, coach and assess operatives in their core tasks and the fundamental Continuous Improvement Tools that are set out in Chapter 5.
5. Ensure that skills matrices that include the photographs of operators and show the current team skill status are shown in production areas. Task line managers with closing their 'skills gap' in their teams (chapter 5, section 13).
6. Create a 'Continuous Improvement Academy' that will enable personnel at all levels of the organisation to acquire and practice Continuous Improvement Skills.
7. Develop a 'Leadership Academy' that will enable the core competencies of first line, middle and senior managers to be developed, implemented and assessed 'on the job.'
8. Train management teams in all the chapters of this manual so that they can deliver and facilitate Continuous Improvement.
9. Meet with your team members on a 1 to 1 basis to review their performance and behavioural development on at least a monthly basis.
10. Ensure that organisational performance development reviews are real (i.e. not just a 'tick box') and are reviewed regularly at the 1 to 1s mentioned above.
11. Mentor senior managers (individuals and teams) to move from being task based 'silo' managers to people-based process managers using an approach based on John Adair's 'Action Centred Leadership' model.

8.1.3 Attitudes

People don't care how much you know until they know how much you care

John C. Maxwell

1. Priority one is to show that you are an authentic manager who is committed to your team's success and the development of your people.
2. Priority two is to be fair, consistent and enthusiastic.
3. Priority three is to ensure that your frontline and middle managers are 'walking the talk' in line with your priorities and are developing their people.
4. Develop and implement a consistent Operational Management system (Chapter 4).

5. Use 'situational based coaching' as the preferred management style for all managers. This will ensure that people are encouraged always to own, make improvements and sort out their own problems as much as possible.

6. Be visible: walk the floor at least once per day if you are a senior manager and more often if you are a middle or frontline manager. Actively review performance and talk with people at their place of work. Manage standards if they are not being met, encourage improvement, say thank you, well done and build trust by asking how they are and how you can help. People will see that you are 'firm but fair' and approachable.

7. Ensure that escalations are encouraged and cascades are always 'closed out' with the 'raiser' even if the answer is no.

8. If operators are moved from their normal position, try to give them fair warning and explain the business reasons why.

9. When talking to people at their place of work, ask how morale is and probe to find out what they think needs to be done to improve it.

10. Know everybody's name in your team and remember an interesting fact from your last conversation to follow up at your next conversation.

11. Never walk in an area with a scowl on your face even if you are having the day from hell!

12. Give people feedback as soon as it has happened so that they can fully recognise good or bad behaviours. Praise in public, criticise in private.

13. When considering change initiatives on the shop floor always follow this mantra: keep it simple; keep it structured; keep it sweet.

14. Ensure that frontline operatives have an opportunity to review performance and hear the latest news from their line managers at least once per day at team 'huddles' or through 'Managing by Walking Around.'

15. Ensure that senior managers face to face brief their frontline teams on the organisation's performance at least once per month including the impact on them.

16. Hold recognition events for individuals, teams and projects.

17. Hold social events with your teams and their families.

18. Use all available media to reinforce the messages above, e.g. Newsletters, table-talkers, posters, TV, etc.

19. It is vital that you encourage a root-cause mind-set and behaviours within the organisation's leaders, teams for both operational reviews and during normal day-to-day working. Please refer to Chapters 4 and 5.

8.1.4 Roles

> Our greatest weakness lies in giving up. The most certain way to
> succeed is always to try just one more time.
>
> **Thomas A. Edison**

> Accountability – It is not only what we do but also what we do not
> do for which we are accountable.
>
> **Moliere**

1. Ensure that people really understand that what is expected of them
   through clear job descriptions that they have been taken through, have
   an input into and 'sign off.'
2. Ensure that performance can be analysed by role from the top of the
   organisation to the shop floor, e.g. Overall Equipment Effectiveness
   (OEE) can be split by factory (Production Manager), plant (Area
   Leader) and then Shift (Team Leader) and then stage in the process
   (Lead Operator). In this way, targets and responsibilities can be clearly
   aligned. Please see Chapter 4.
3. Ensure that all roles include responsibilities and time for training, development and Continuous Improvement. The more senior the role the
   greater the proportion of time should be spent on these.
4. Senior Managers should become Leaders – follow 'Action Centred'
   Leadership and promote its use with their teams. Their 'role modelling'
   will propagate through the teams and encourage people to take ownership (Figure 8.3).

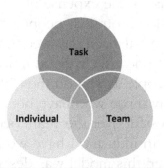

Figure 8.3　John Adair's 'Action Centred' leadership.

John Adair came up with a leadership model that suggested that if a leader does not spend equal amounts of effort (time and focus) on the 'task,' the 'team' together and the 'individuals' in their team respectively, that he will not be effective. Examples of each area:

- **Task:** Routine review meetings with other senior managers; preparing performance related budgets, plans and reports; 'troubleshooting' problems and issues; unplanned requests; ensuring that standards are developed and in place for all their team's processes and activities; ensuring that there are performance measures, processes and reviews in place to monitor and improve performance; developing and executing performance improvement activities, general administration etc.
- **Team:** Team meetings, team briefings, reviewing skills gaps in their team and developing training plans, working with performance improvement teams as a facilitator and/or coach, team building events, socialising with the team, holding recognition events, developing a long-term plan for the development of the team structure with clear succession plans etc.
- **Individual:** 'Managing by walking around'- talking (performance review and informal) to people at their place of work, regular 1 to 1s with team members to review performance and development, informal chats over cup of tea/coffee, developing and regularly reviewing personal development plans for all their team members that align with both the company's and their team member's aspirations, effective recruitment, counselling, managing and investigating absence, managing conduct, holding disciplinary reviews, etc.

Typically, poorly performing managers fall into two camps: They either excessively focus on the task at the expense of their people (individuals and teams) or they excessively focus on their people at the expense of the task. The effective manager has a balanced day/week/month and year.

The key insight is that to be effective you must spend twice as much time and effort on your people as you do the task. This is extremely hard for some people, especially those who have been promoted to their role and been personally successful over the years because they are good with the 'task.' During my time in industry, I have worked with many such leaders and typical replies when this model was described to them were as follows:

■ I would really like to do this but when am I going to get the time, I am just too busy with other things (e.g. breakdowns, staff problems, work that the boss has asked him to do, requests from head office, HR requests).
■ Isn't all the 'fluffy stuff' HR's responsibility?
■ If other people left me in peace then I would get around to it.
■ My people just want to be left to get on with the job; they are not interested in this and just want to come into work for the money.

It takes a brave leader to accept that their fundamental role is to build their teams to deliver today and solve their own problems which releases them, the leader, to spend time thinking, networking, planning and developing the team for tomorrow's challenges.

How to get there:

i. Believe that to be successful in your role that it is 'all about people.'
ii. Develop a clear vision for your role and your team for the next 12 months. Why does the role exist? What are the priorities? How will you be spending your day? Trust your team with delivery.
iii. For a couple of weeks, monitor your working week and see where your time is going by using the task, team, individual sub-categories above. Is there an equal split between the three areas and if there is not is it because of:
   a. Poor time management, e.g. too much time working on urgent rather than important matters.
   b. 'Troubleshooting' plant or product or process or people issues.
   c. Having to do your team member's tasks because of poor capability and/or absence and/or lack of standards/processes.
   d. Unexpected demands from your boss.
   e. Unexpected demands from your colleagues.
   f. Unexpected demands from outside the organisation.
   g. Tasks taking longer than originally envisaged.
iv. From your analysis develop corrective measures to address both immediate and longer-term issues. Discuss with your line manager.
v. Develop a four-week rolling plan where you ensure that task, team and individual activities are scheduled to give you the balance you need. Allow time for unplanned activities and 'thinking time.'
vi. Really try to stick to the plan and act assertively to 'protect it.'
vii. If you are unable to do things, record why and get down to root-cause to address them.

8.1.5 Technology

1. The plant and processes that we operate must, of course, must have sufficient 'capability' to meet the demands of customers in terms of quality and service. Improvements to plant and processes can be achieved using various processes, e.g. 5S, basic problem solving, DMAIC and set-up reduction (please refer to Chapter 5 and 7) however we should not forget the reliability of the processes in the first place and the implementation of the various stages of Total Productive Maintenance (TPM) is key to this (Chapter 7) starting off with robust Planned Preventative Maintenance and 'Asset Care' by operators including Cleaning, Inspection and Lubrication. As always, the key aspect is ownership backed up with good measures and reviews that are driven and continuously improved by the team.

8.1.6 Systems

1. Think 'systemically' rather than 'silo.' The Managing behaviour model in Figure 8.2 shows that each area impacts others in some way.
2. Develop Operational Management systems (Chapter 4) that enable performance to be tracked and analysed in real time, i.e. provide the operator and all management levels with instant feedback of 'how the line is performing' this hour/shift/day/week/month year with associated root causes. Really focus on who needs what information to make decisions and take actions rather than merely generating reports for the next level up.
3. Implement the Operational Management system (Chapter 4) with top-down commitment and bottom up implementation: pull rather than push!
4. Implement a standards-based culture through **Standard Routines** as described in Chapter 5.

By doing this, we will move from a 'feedback control' to a 'feedforward' culture, which is illustrated by the following story:

Back in the late 1980s, when I was a (very!) young process engineer working for a pet food manufacturer, I was given the opportunity of attending a food processing seminar in Birmingham. The agenda was full of a whole array of papers describing new and improved process engineering techniques and control methods and I settled down with a pencil poised to listen and learn. The first few topics were earnest descriptions of new processing methods but essentially dull and left me yawning and looking out of the window at a beautiful spring day.

The droning voice of the last speaker eventually stopped and I joined everyone in a polite round of applause. I then looked down to see what suitably gripping topic was up next. My interest was piqued when I read the words 'New Developments in Food Process Quality Control' as this was potentially relevant to a problem that I had with my current main project. However, I really had no inkling about what I was about to hear would change my outlook on my work for ever and was the start of my ongoing passion for people development and all things to do with Continuous Improvement.

What was the context for this epiphany? At the time, I was involved in the development of new processes for new petfood products. This essentially involved scaling up products that had originally been designed and made by hand on the laboratory bench to a full-scale production line. The main project I was working on at the time would shortly involve asking the factory to install new chunk making equipment, mixers, pumps and fillers. My mindset was to design the kit effectively and all will be well – technology is the answer! The point that was troubling me was that many of our existing brands, which were made in the factory that the new product was destined for, were hugely different in appearance to the same product when it was made in the development laboratory. The latter would typically look and smell very appetising from a pet owners' point of view whereas the factory version would smell the same but look like an 'emulsified mush.' At the time, products were mainly a 'matrix format' in cans, so customers were not aware of this difference. However, as this new product was a completely new chunk in gravy format – it was a real concern that the chunks which we had made with such loving care would be literally smashed up during the handling process. I had been in discussion with the factory management regarding moving to new forms of gentle handling processes, but they were very reticent about changing to 'kit that would not be robust enough' – we had a real mountain to climb to convince them. To address these concerns, how could we develop an automatic product quality control system that would monitor the quality of the final product and then make the necessary adjustments to the process settings to ensure we controlled the quality and protected the equipment if it went out of tolerance. This 'feedback control' method is illustrated in Figure 8.4.

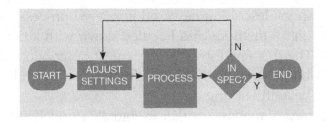

Figure 8.4 Feedback control. Source: The Chemical Engineer October 2018.

Returning to the seminar, the speaker had begun to describe a very similar diagram to that above and I was reassured that we were on the right track. He then said something that I did not expect – indeed he said it twice for maximum effect. It was essentially that measuring a food process output and then trying to control the quality of complex food attributes (like appearance) in real time is essentially a waste of time and effort because by the time you have detected products moving out of specification it is too late to correct them. He said that as there were generally so many contributing factors it was very difficult to distinguish quickly what process condition had caused the problem in the first place and to make an adjustment before you had made lots of below par or to even reject product.

He said that solution was 'feedforward' control where the inputs to the process are all understood and controlled to make sure the output quality is assured. He described the benefits of such an approach to be immense but said the barriers to achieving it were legion not least because it required a change of culture. It involved designing out failure and moving to an environment of 'proactiveness, calmness and light' as opposed to 'reactiveness, heat and noise.' His experience was that many managers opposed this approach as it suggested their troubleshooting skills and, by definition, their roles would not be needed. He ended his talk with the proposal that the future of food process quality control lay in the development of standards developed and maintained by multidisciplinary teams of end users and experts (Figure 8.5).

Four main steps had to be followed:

i. Identify and develop the right standards with end users and experts through rigorous design and approval – involve and develop people.
ii. Accurately train out all users in the application of the standards –involve and develop people.
iii. Continuously coach users in the application of the standards – involve and develop people,

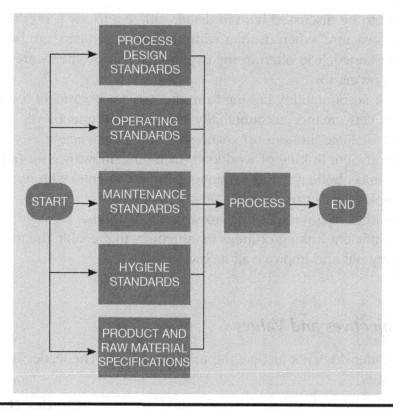

Figure 8.5   Feedforward control. Source: The Chemical Engineer October 2018.

iv. Drive for improvement of results and continuously improve the standards – involve and develop people.

The message was standards are 'king' and standards are owned and developed by people with the most important people in this equation being the people who use them. The manager's role would need to change to ensuring that people had the right skills and capabilities to develop and improve their own standards – he called this a sustainable Continuous Improvement culture. We also now know this process by the term Standard Routines (Chapter 5, Section 5.13).

I came away with an idea in my mind that standards were the way forward and that achieving very high performance was all about people.

8.1.7 Structure

1. The organisational structure and the roles of a company can be adapted through Organisational Development (OD) which is far too large a

subject to be discussed here in detail, suffice it to say it is critical to think 'structure' when dealing with how improvements can be made and sustained. Too often in my experience improvements are not sustained owing to:

a. Poor accountability linking from the 'top' to 'bottom' of a company. E.g. Performance accountability stops at department level. This does not facilitate 'bottom-up' ownership and improvement.

b. Insufficient linking of workload (including allowance for training, absence, holidays, and continuous improvements) with number of employees to carry it out.

c. Insufficient linking of roles to structure to skills.

d. Insufficient linking of areas to structures that enable the team to carry out and improve all its own work.

8.1.8 Objectives and Values

> The leader does not just get the message across. The leader is the message.
>
> **Charles Handy**

In the introduction of this manual, it was postulated that the reason that many organisations fail to implement and sustain a Continuous Improvement culture is owing to a failure of leadership.

Many organisations have values or principles statements which when you discuss with the frontline teams, they do not understand them, seeing them at best as something that does not relate to their daily work and at worst something that demotivates them as it clearly does not represent what is happening 'on the ground.'

Within this manual we have discussed the importance of system thinking in two primary areas: Operational Management and Strategy Deployment. Effective implementation and sustaining of these is how values and objectives are linked to the behaviours of people on a day to day basis. Leadership's role is to ensure that these processes are designed, installed and used in the ways described in Chapters 4 and 7 of this manual. If they do not then it will not take long for the processes to atrophy and the culture to 'go backwards.' Once this happens, it will make things harder in the future for future leaders to implement as the team will remember that 'it did not work last time.'

Regarding values or principles does the Senior Leadership Team fully understand the following:

Who is responsible for performance and the behaviours within an organisation? The answer is:

8.1.9 Leaders!

Professor Edgar Schein of the MIT Sloan School of Management said:

> The only thing of real importance that leaders do is to create and manage culture. If you do not manage culture, it manages you, and you may not even be aware of the extent to which this is happening.

If they do not, then there is work to be done through working as a team to identify what their values or principles are and how well the organisation is 'living them' on daily basis with the help of a Senior Continuous Improvement Practitioner or 'Sensei,' a Japanese word for someone who has achieved mastery of their subject and is a teacher.

The Sensei will work with the team and facilitate the development of their values, what it required to put them into practice and develop a plan.

In terms of examples of Values/Principles it is worth considering 'The Toyota Way' and the *Shingo Model*™, respectively:

Toyota's management principles are clearly set out in 'The Toyota Way' by Jeff Liker (McGraw Hill 2021).

1. Base your management decisions on long-term systems thinking, even at the expense of short-term financial goals.
2. Connect people and processes through continuous process flow to bring problems to the surface.
3. Use 'pull' systems to avoid overproduction.
4. Level out the workload, like the tortoise, not the hare (Heijunka).
5. Work to establish standardised processes as the foundation for Continuous Improvement.
6. Build a culture of stopping to identify out of standard conditions and build in quality.
7. Use visual control to support people in decision making and problem solving.
8. Adopt and adapt technology that supports your people and processes.

9. Grow leaders who thoroughly understand the work, live the philosophy, and teach it to others.
10. Develop exceptional people and teams who follow your company's philosophy.
11. Respect your value chain partners and suppliers by challenging them and helping them improve.
12. Observe deeply and learn iteratively (PDCA) to meet each challenge.
13. Focus the improvement energy of your people through aligned goals at all levels..
14. Learn your way to the future through bold strategy, some large leaps and many small steps.

The *Shingo Model*™ can be described under the following headings:

1. Guiding Principles.
2. Systems.
3. Tools.
4. Results.
5. Culture.

Further information can be found in *Discover Excellence: An Overview of the Shingo Model and Its Guiding Principles* by Gerard J. Plenert (Productivity Press 2017).

If the senior management team are 'not ready' for the above and there is a desire from one leader to 'just get on with it.' How can this be done without compromising the long-term sustainability of the improvements and cultural aspirations?

In Chapter 3, I discussed the importance of a Business Analysis to start off because implementing a Continuous Improvement Way of Working ('culture') is not a destination, it is a journey. The Business Analysis will provide the business case for implementing Continuous Improvement within the context of the organisation's strategy or perhaps just within the context of some local challenges.

For the plan coming out of the Business Analysis to be successful each of the criteria set out in the following change table, which was shown in Chapter 2, needs to be achieved (Table 8.1).

Top leadership engagement in the governance of change which is essentially ensuring that each of the items in Table 8.1 are attended to on a

Table 8.1 Continuous Improvement Checklist

Item	Comments	Achieved (Yes or No?)
Situation	An awareness of where you are at the moment and any shortfalls.	
Motive	There is desire to leave where you are at the moment and go to where you want to be.	
Destination	Know where you are going: the 'target condition.'	
Capability	Have the means and opportunity to get there: resources, time, skills and tools .	
Route Map	Plan the work, work the plan.	

routine basis is key. The subsequent implementation and maintenance of the Operational Management system and the Strategy Deployment System will ensure this happens.

8.2 How to Check If the Organisation Is Ready?

This is a question that is often asked by senior leaders: 'We'd love to do Continuous Improvement but we're just too busy at the moment.' I would respectfully claim that what they really mean is 'We're really, really busy, we don't really understand or appreciate what's involved and its benefits, I'm worried about today (and my survival) let alone tomorrow and so therefore I do not see it as priority!'

I have also been in situations where a senior leaders has said one of the following:

■ We need to get some stability first before we go onto the next stage.
■ I need to have the right people in place before we start.
■ There are too many moving parts at the moment.
■ Let's get the Capital Expenditure project finished first.
■ Sales are too high at the moment.

In essence, the organisation is always ready for Continuous Improvement because it is an essential part of managing an organisation

To convince leaders, the recommendation is to use Table 8.1: if the answer is 'no' to any of the items, then you are ready to do Continuous Improvement by defining and putting in place each of them. By defining the plan, at least you know what needs to be done and what the benefits will be. If the answer is 'yes' to all of them then carry on! If in doubt, carry out a 'Business Analysis' (Chapter 3); this will define what needs to be done with a 'go' or 'no go' decision at the end.

It can be a 'hard sell' to convince a senior team that they need to think in a new way particularly as they are, by definition of where they are, successful individuals. A 'Sensei' can work with the team over a period to persuade them of the benefits of this new way of working. Please also see section 10 in this chapter.

8.3 What If Continuous Improvement Has Failed a Few Times?

Continuous Improvement is hardly rocket science and has been around in one form or another since the start of human civilisation. That being said, there is still a tendency particularly within Western countries to see it as 'that area with a lot of Japanese words' or bolt on a bit like health and safety was seen at one time, i.e. something that applies to experts but not me.

From my experience, where CI has failed in the past, it is that it has been treated as separate function or some tools to be added onto the day job and not treated as an integral part of the same and/or a lower priority 'nice to have' that then just gets overlooked as the initial enthusiasm wanes. If you think of CI as 'oxygen' and think of the day job as 'life on earth,' I am sure you will appreciate the priority that I think should be given to Continuous Improvement within organisations!

In organisations where there have been failures in the past, the advice is to ensure that the change is properly governed using Table 8.1 plus to start small and build from there. The Operational Management system model described in Chapter 4 is recommended; this bottom up approach will produce immediate results and create an environment of success that will beget further success.

The role of the Sensei working with the Senior Leadership Team, as described in Section 8.1.9 under Objectives and Values, will also be extremely important. Without strong leadership, CI will quickly atrophy and eventually fizzle out.

8.4 How Do I Know I'm Keeping to the Right Direction?

The development and implementation of the Strategy Deployment process will ensure this is adequately covered, please refer to Chapter 6.

8.5 How Do I Hook in All the Departments?

Very often Continuous Improvement starts in the Value Adding Departments such as the Production team (consider Figure 8.6)

In this example Production has started without involving the other functions at all. As many of the issues will involve other departments, and for long-term sustainability, it is much better to have an approach that involves them through communication and involvement in projects and activities. This could be properly governed through the Strategy Deployment process (Chapter 6). This approach is shown in Figure 8.7.

Even better is a 'wall to wall, floor to ceiling' approach that typically follows after the successes in the main value adding Department (Figure 8.8).

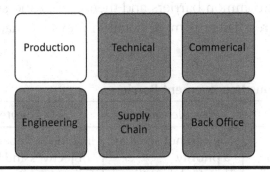

Figure 8.6   CI in one department only.

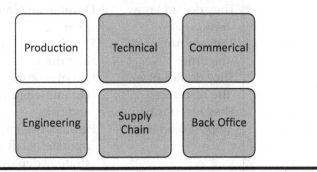

Figure 8.7   CI in one department only with involvement of other departments.

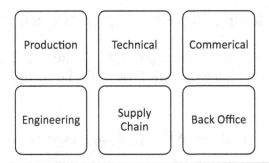

Figure 8.8   CI in all departments.

8.6 Creating the Right Environment.

The Operational Management System and Strategy Deployment approaches described in Chapters 4 and 6 will ensure that this occurs. Continuous Improvement requires a cadence – these processes provide this

8.7 Barriers

These are the most common barriers and their causes and suggestions of possible countermeasures. There is more detail in previous chapters (Table 8.2).

Table 8.2   Continuous Improvement Barriers

Barrier	Possible Causes	Countermeasures
Leaders, Managers and Frontline Team member do not participate in CI	They do not see it as a priority. They feel threatened by it. They do not know how. They do not have the time. They do not have the resources. They feel it is being imposed on them.	Include in department, annual objectives and budget. Communication of the philosophy and benefits. Develop and implement a training plan. Develop structures and ensure it is a priority. Use of monthly review or steering committee to escalate obstacles and risks Participative implementation of operational management and strategy deployment systems.

(Continued)

Table 8.2 (Continued)   Continuous Improvement Barriers

Barrier	Possible Causes	Countermeasures
There is a lack of awareness of the business benefits of a CI way of working	People only know what they know. People see it as a lower priority.	Develop and implement a training plan. Include in department, annual objectives and budget.
Reticence to start CI	No clear business case. Previous failures of CI. Too much on. Perception it is a 'nice to have' as opposed to a 'crucial' part of work.	Undertake Business Analysis to develop plan. Robust implementation of operational management and strategy deployment systems. Communication of the philosophy and benefits.
Operational Management and strategy deployment Systems are not adhered to	Too much on. People see it as a low priority.	Include in department, annual objectives and budget. Communication of the philosophy and benefits. Robust implementation of operational management and strategy deployment systems.
People do not have enough time to work on CI projects and Activities	Effective plan has not been developed. Sponsorship is poor. Managers do not see it as priority.	Effective governance and sponsorship through toll gate process, QUAD reports and CI plan monthly or weekly reviews. Sponsor training. Include in department and annual objectives.
Losses are not readily identified	Poor data capture. Lack of training.	Implementation of effective data capture systems. Develop and implement a training plan.

8.8 The Application of Psychology

Within the methods used in this manual we have focused on 'acting our way into a new way of thinking,' i.e. start doing different things and this will promote new thoughts which in turn generate feelings which will reinforce the behaviours.

Consider the following cycle (Figure 8.9).

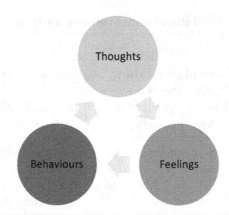

Figure 8.9 Thoughts, feelings, behaviour cycle.

This is different to a more 'academic' way of learning where we teach people in the abstract with concepts with the hope that they will then put them into practice.

The Operational Management System and Strategy Deployment System are essentially a framework of behaviours that combined with strong leadership will ensure that a Continuous Improvement culture becomes embedded within a company. This goes back to W. Edwards Deming's famous quotation:

> 85% of the reasons for failure are deficiencies in the systems and process rather than the employee. The role of management is to change the process rather than badgering individuals to do better.

Through the achievement of small wins on a daily basis, the leaders and teams will become convinced that CI processes are the only way and so it will become embedded as 'the way things are done around here.'

The key to this is to practice the skills as one would do when learning a new musical instrument or a new sport. The role of the line manager becoming a coach is central to this approach; the GROW model discussed in Chapter 4 is an excellent framework. if you ask people to make small improvements, they will, given the right levels of support and guidance.

8.9 Use of Consultants

Ultimately sustainable Continuous Improvement should be undertaken by people who do the job so why use Consultants?

Consultants provide the following benefits:

■ They are experts in their field who have a knowledge of the latest best practices and approaches.
■ They can work with senior leaders to help them understand the philosophies of sustainable Continuous Improvement and the benefits it can bring.
■ They will be able to help you develop an effective strategy through Business Analysis without 'fear or favour.'
■ They are able to see things with 'a fresh pair of eyes' and point out opportunities with the local team who may have become blind to the issues and opportunities available.
■ They will create a 'sense of urgency' and, combined with a structured approach, be able to introduce new methods and deliver business benefits at a much higher speed than if the local team had undertaken matters on their own.
■ They can show how 'all the pieces fit together' and facilitate the development of coherent Continuous Improvement capability building through training and coaching that will ultimately give the team the skills to carry on, on their own.
■ They will challenge the status quo and remove barriers to progress.
■ They can stay separate from any departmental 'politics.'

It is important to select consultants whose aim is to implement sustainable Continuous Improvement cultures and who share your values; there has to be a fit. Those that claim to be CI Consultants and promise quick wins in ways that 'cut and burn' are consultants but *are not* following a CI philosophy.

8.10 How to Sell Lean to the Food Industry

Source: The Chemical Engineer March 2019

IMAGINE you are a sales executive and you have been given the job of selling an extraordinary machine to senior executives within the food industry. This machine does not produce any food product but has the capability to not only turn every $1 you put into it to at least $3 within a year but also to make your organisation better in terms of safety, quality and delivery performance with a substantially more motivated and engaged workforce.

The machine is not new, although it is massively improved; its founding principles have been around since the end of the Second World War. So you'd be forgiven for assuming that every food company must have one by now and that there would be very few customers for it left.

Imagine further that I tell you that there is still a huge opportunity and that the take up is surprisingly low. So what is this machine? This 'machine' is Lean Manufacturing (see Figure 8.10). Of course, it is a philosophy rather than an actual machine but as a system of behaviours and methodologies, I think 'machine' is a good way to describe it. I add that many of your prospective customers will have heard of it and, indeed, many will have tried it and either adopted it in a fairly limited manner or reverted back to their previous ways of doing things after a fairly short while. I'm afraid that selling the Lean Manufacturing machine to the food industry is a hard sell, but I have some tips that will help you.

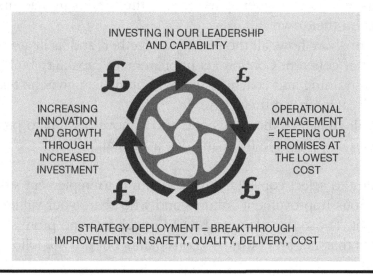

INVESTING IN OUR LEADERSHIP AND CAPABILITY

INCREASING INNOVATION AND GROWTH THROUGH INCREASED INVESTMENT

OPERATIONAL MANAGEMENT = KEEPING OUR PROMISES AT THE LOWEST COST

STRATEGY DEPLOYMENT = BREAKTHROUGH IMPROVEMENTS IN SAFETY, QUALITY, DELIVERY, COST

Figure 8.10   The Lean 'Flywheel.'

8.10.1 *Where Do You Start?*

Assuming they are interested in the business case described above, first ask the senior executive to complete the checklist in Figure 8.11. What happens if they answer 'no' to any of the questions or are not sure? Explain to them that before they progress any further they (the senior management team) have to achieve a solid 'yes' to all of the questions. Tell them they will need to work with a Lean teacher (or 'sensei') to teach them about Lean principles and how to think differently. The sensei will

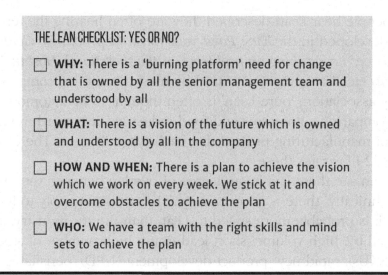

THE LEAN CHECKLIST: YES OR NO?

☐ **WHY:** There is a 'burning platform' need for change that is owned by all the senior management team and understood by all

☐ **WHAT:** There is a vision of the future which is owned and understood by all in the company

☐ **HOW AND WHEN:** There is a plan to achieve the vision which we work on every week. We stick at it and overcome obstacles to achieve the plan

☐ **WHO:** We have a team with the right skills and mind sets to achieve the plan

Figure 8.11   The Lean Checklist.

convince them that they will need to change their behaviours because without their leadership, continuing involvement and discipline, the whole Lean implementation will fail.

8.10.2 Lean – Isn't that Just for Car Manufacture?

No. And a little bit of history might help here. Lean, although a philosophy which was arguably first described by Womack, Jones and Roos in the early 1990s, has its origins in the approach started by Deming in Japan in the 1940s. By the late 1970s, the relative success of the Japanese manufacturing industry compared to the West's (the so-called 'Japanese Miracle') was being dissected by Western companies, particularly automotive who were, at that stage, being soundly beaten on quality, reliability and price.

The approach at that stage was called Total Quality Management, or Kaizen. It principally entailed focussing on Continuous Improvement of processes through frontline worker involvement. Well known techniques that were developed included: 5S; simplified flows and material layouts; autonomous maintenance; standardised work; just in time; visual management and controls; and set up reduction (single minute exchange of dies – SMED).

Toyota took this approach to another level with the Toyota Production System (TPS). This philosophy was the one essentially described by Womack, Jones and Roos, and involves the following guiding principles: Value; The Value Stream; Flow; Pull; and Perfection.

When people hear Lean described they are often hearing the terms that were developed in the TPS: *Poka-yoke (mistake proofing), Gemba ('the real place,' i.e. working on problems on the shop floor), Hoshin (Policy Deployment)* etc. These terms are used by most automotive companies these days so, by association, 'pure Lean' is often thought to be automotive.

When comparing automotive and food industries, it is worth reviewing the types of manufacturing process that each typically uses. The continuum in Figure 8.12 illustrates these.

As you can see there is a large degree of overlap between the two industries so 'technically' there is no reason why Lean cannot apply to food. In actual fact it is probably more suited to Lean than the car industry, as it is characterised by: high volume; short lead times; high number of stock keeping units (SKUs); rapid new product development (NPD), perishable products; multiple retailer requirements; and defined manufacturing processes.

The demands of the automotive and traditional engineering assembly industry are in fact moving in this direction. The high number of product variations required by 'mass customisation' is, in essence, exposing their manufacturing operations more to the demands of the marketplace by removing the safety (and cost) of finished goods inventory. Within the chilled food industry, in particular, this has long been a fact of life because companies cannot hold large amounts of finished goods stock because of the risk of the product going past its shelf life.

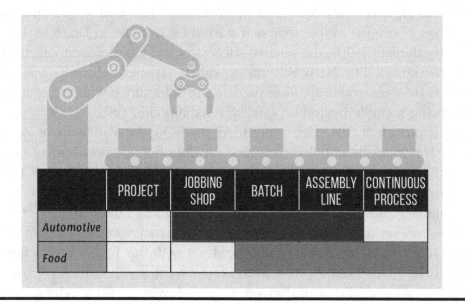

	PROJECT	JOBBING SHOP	BATCH	ASSEMBLY LINE	CONTINUOUS PROCESS
Automotive					
Food					

Figure 8.12 Process continuum.

It is also interesting to note that a lot of the Lean work in automotive component operations has involved 'identifying the value stream.' This is because many companies still have a workshop set up, e.g. a foundry, a machine shop, a paint shop, a fabrication area, an assembly shop etc. This means that they had very little concept of the processes for individual products and parts, for instance, could be in the system for months and even years. This typically does not apply to the food industry where product comes in one end of the factory and literally goes in a pipe or along a belt until it is finished. The processes are much easier to see and 'parts' are in the system for a matter of hours or days.

8.10.3 Go and See

If your senior executives are still not convinced then ask them to go and see for themselves. There are many world-class companies who are willing to show interested parties around, to talk to people who live and breathe Lean on a daily basis. They recognise that such visits are a win-win activity that will not only give benefits to the visitors but they will learn something new too. Above all else, it is this enthusiasm and drive for progress and improvement and respect for people which underpins their culture which the visitors will experience and take away from such a visit. Their financial results will also speak for themselves.

There are many world-class companies who are willing to show interested parties around, to talk to people who live and breathe Lean on a daily basis. The prospective customer may then ask what needs to be done to make a Lean enterprise sustainable. My advice would be to ask them to picture a three-legged stool (see Figure 8.13).

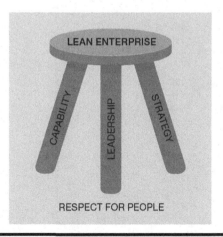

Figure 8.13　The Lean enterprise as a three-legged stool.

We all know that a stool is a very stable seat but if you take away one of the legs it will fall over.

First and foremost, it is a culture that is built on respect for people.

Secondly, there is leadership at all levels to not only to stick to improved ways of doing things by rigorous adherence to standards but also to lead and develop teams to achieve success for both the business and themselves.

Thirdly, there must be a continually-refined strategy built on Lean principles that is aligned with the business priorities that everyone plays their part in achieving. Finally, it is about a never-ending focus on building both Lean methodology and leadership capability. With all these elements in place, Lean will be sustained and it has only one enemy – pride (and we all know what comes after pride!).

Bibliography

1. Out of the Crisis – W. Edwards Deming (MIT Press 1986).
2. The Machine that Changed the World – James P. Womack, Daniel T. Jones and Daniel Roos (Simon and Schuster 1991).
3. The Toyota Way – Jeff Liker (McGraw Hill 2021).
4. Lean Six Sigma and Minitab – Quentin Brook (Opex Resources 2014).
5. The Toyota Engagement Equation – Tracey and Ernie Richardson (McGraw Hill 2017).
6. A Manual for Change – Terry Wilson (Gower 1994).
7. The Lean Tool Box – John Bicheno, Matthias Holweg (PICSIE Books 2016).
8. The Spirit of Kaizen – Robert Maurer (McGraw Hill 2013).
9. The Lean Six Sigma Pocket Book – Michael George, David Rowlands, Mark Price, John Maxey (George Group 2005).
10. The Goal – Eliyahu M. Goldratt and Jeff Cox (Gower 2004).
11. The Toyota Kata Practice Guide – Mike Rother (McGraw Hill 2018).
12. TPM for Every Operator – Japanese Institute of Plant Management (Productivity Press 1996).
13. Lean RFS (Repetitive Flexible Supply Ian Glenday and Rick Sather (Productivity Press 2013).
14. The 7 Habits of Highly Effective People – Stephen Covey (Simon and Schuster 1989).
15. Our Iceberg Is Melting – John Kotter and Holger Rathgeber (MacMillan 2005).
16. Discover Excellence: An overview of the Shingo Model and Its Guiding Principles – Gerard J. Plenert (Productivity Press 2017).
17. Fundamentals of Preventive Maintenance – John M. Goss (Amacom 2006).

Recommended for DMAIC Belt Training with Certification

Torrs Consulting Ltd
Claudius Consulting Ltd

Table 9.1 Links to Chapters

Chapter/Area	Book
Business analysis	9
Operational management facilitation	3, 7
Fundamental continuous improvement tools	8, 9
Strategy deployment facilitation	7, 10
Improvement activities and projects	4, 5, 7, 8, 9, 11, 12, 13, 17
Skills and culture development	1, 2, 3, 6, 7, 14, 15, 16

Table 9.2 Links to Methodologies

Method	Book
DMAIC	4
A3 thinking	5
TPM	12

Index

Printed in the United States
by Baker & Taylor Publisher Services

Printed in the United States
by Baker & Taylor Publisher Services